THE COMPLETE GUIDE TO LINUX FOR PROGRAMMERS

Learn Linux Commands, Shell Scripting, and System Administration

THOMPSON CARTER

TABLE OF CONTENTS

Introduction

Linux, the open-source operating system, has become the backbone of modern technology, revolutionizing the way developers create, deploy, and manage software. From web servers to mobile devices, supercomputers to IoT devices, Linux powers a vast majority of the world's computing infrastructure. It's not just an operating system; it's a thriving ecosystem that fosters innovation, efficiency, and freedom.

This book, *The Complete Guide to Linux for Programmers: Learn Linux Commands, Shell Scripting, and System Administration*, is designed to serve as a comprehensive resource for programmers, software developers, and tech enthusiasts who want to leverage the full potential of Linux. Whether you're a beginner taking your first steps in the Linux environment or an experienced developer seeking to refine your skills, this book provides practical insights, real-world examples, and actionable knowledge tailored to meet your needs.

Why Linux Matters for Programmers

Linux is more than just a choice of operating system for developers; it's a tool that enables creativity and productivity. Here are a few reasons why Linux is indispensable for programmers:

1. **Versatility**: Linux supports a wide range of programming languages, development environments, and tools, making it ideal for projects ranging from simple scripts to large-scale enterprise applications.

2. **Stability and Performance**: Known for its reliability, Linux is often the go-to platform for deploying applications in production environments.

3. **Cost-Effectiveness**: As an open-source system, Linux eliminates licensing costs, making it accessible for developers and organizations alike.

4. **Community and Innovation**: Backed by a vibrant community, Linux evolves rapidly, offering cutting-edge technologies for modern programming needs.

What You'll Learn

This book is structured to take you on a journey through the foundational concepts of Linux and progressively guide you toward mastering advanced topics. Key areas of focus include:

- **Linux Basics**: Understand the Linux operating system, its history, and its significance in modern computing.

- **Command-Line Proficiency**: Learn essential commands to navigate the Linux file system, manage processes, and manipulate data efficiently.

- **Shell Scripting**: Master the art of automation with powerful Bash scripts that streamline repetitive tasks and improve workflow efficiency.

- **System Administration**: Gain practical knowledge in managing users, permissions, services, and network configurations on Linux systems.

- **Development Tools**: Discover how to set up programming environments, use version control systems, and optimize Linux for specific development needs.

- **Real-World Projects**: Build hands-on experience with practical examples, from deploying web servers to automating CI/CD pipelines and managing cloud instances.

Each chapter includes step-by-step tutorials, examples, and exercises to help solidify your understanding and provide practical experience with Linux.

Who Should Read This Book
This book is crafted with a wide audience in mind:

1. **Beginners**: If you are new to Linux, this book offers a gentle introduction, focusing on practical examples and eliminating unnecessary jargon.

2. **Intermediate Developers**: Those with basic Linux knowledge will find advanced topics like shell scripting, system administration, and performance tuning valuable.

3. **Experienced Programmers**: Developers seeking to deepen their Linux expertise or learn emerging technologies like containerization and cloud computing will benefit from this book's comprehensive coverage.

Whether you're a student, a professional developer, or a tech hobbyist, this book provides tools and knowledge that are critical to success in today's tech landscape.

Why This Book Is Unique

1. **Jargon-Free Explanations**: Technical concepts are broken down into simple, easy-to-understand language, making Linux accessible to everyone.

2. **Real-World Examples**: The book is packed with practical scenarios and projects that reflect the challenges developers face in the real world.

3. **Step-by-Step Learning**: Each topic is presented in a logical sequence, building a strong foundation before moving on to advanced concepts.

4. **Diverse Topics**: From basic commands to cloud computing and DevOps practices, this book covers the full spectrum of Linux programming and system administration.

How to Use This Book

To get the most out of this book, follow these tips:

- **Read Actively**: Follow along with examples and try out commands on your own Linux system. Use a virtual machine or a cloud instance if needed.
- **Practice Regularly**: Work through the exercises at the end of each chapter to reinforce your learning.
- **Experiment**: Explore variations of the examples provided. Linux is a flexible system, and experimentation is a great way to learn.
- **Build Projects**: Use the real-world projects in this book as templates to create your own, tailoring them to your specific needs.

What Lies Ahead

By the end of this book, you will have a solid grasp of Linux programming, system administration, and automation. You will be equipped to:

- Develop, deploy, and manage applications on Linux systems.
- Build robust, automated workflows using shell scripting and DevOps tools.
- Troubleshoot and optimize Linux systems for performance and reliability.
- Stay ahead of emerging trends in Linux and open-source technologies.

The journey begins now. Embrace the power of Linux, unlock your programming potential, and take your skills to new heights.

Let's dive in!

Chapter 1: Introduction to Linux

1.1 Overview of Linux: History and Evolution

1. **The Origin of Unix and the Birth of Linux**
   - o Brief history of Unix: How it inspired Linux
   - o Key milestones: Development of the GNU Project by Richard Stallman
   - o The story of Linus Torvalds: Creation of the Linux kernel in 1991

2. **Linux's Open-Source Philosophy**
   - o Explanation of open-source principles
   - o The role of the Free Software Foundation (FSF) and the GPL license
   - o The global impact of open-source contributions

3. **Major Developments in Linux Over the Decades**
   - o Key versions of the Linux kernel
   - o Integration of Linux into servers, desktops, mobile devices, and IoT
   - o How Linux became the foundation for Android

4. **Linux Today: A Powerhouse for Modern Technology**
   - o Linux's role in enterprise systems and cloud computing
   - o Widespread adoption in supercomputers and data centers

o How Linux powers everyday tools like routers and smart devices

---

1.2 Key Features of Linux: Why Programmers Should Use It

1. **Reliability and Stability**
   o Explanation of why Linux rarely crashes
   o Case studies of Linux uptime records in servers and enterprises
2. **Security Features**
   o Built-in security tools: SELinux, AppArmor, and firewalls
   o The role of permissions and process isolation
3. **Customizability and Flexibility**
   o Overview of desktop environments (GNOME, KDE, XFCE)
   o How Linux allows users to build tailored solutions
4. **Rich Development Ecosystem**
   o Pre-installed programming tools and compilers
   o Availability of robust package managers for installing libraries
5. **Community Support and Resources**
   o How the Linux community contributes to its growth

o Forums, documentation, and open-source repositories

6. **Free and Open Source**

o Eliminating licensing costs for programmers and businesses

o Examples of companies thriving using open-source solutions

1.3 Setting Up a Linux Environment

1. **Choosing the Right Linux Distribution**

o Overview of beginner-friendly distros (Ubuntu, Fedora)

o Advanced distros for specific use cases (Debian, Arch Linux)

o Tips for selecting a distro based on development needs

2. **Installing Linux on Different Systems**

o Detailed guide for installing Linux on a dedicated machine

o Setting up Linux as a dual-boot system with Windows or macOS

o Running Linux on virtual machines using VirtualBox or VMware

3. **Live USB and Persistent Installation**

   o   How to create a Linux Live USB for testing

   o   Setting up a persistent Linux USB for portability

4. **Configuring Linux Post-Installation**

   o   Setting up user accounts and managing privileges

   o   Updating and upgrading the system for the first time

   o   Installing essential drivers and software

5. **Exploring the Linux Desktop Environment**

   o   Introduction to GNOME, KDE, and lightweight alternatives

   o   Customizing the desktop: Themes, extensions, and layouts

6. **Familiarizing Yourself with the Linux Terminal**

   o   Introduction to the shell: Bash and alternatives (Zsh, Fish)

   o   Basic terminal navigation: Commands like ls, cd, pwd, and man

   o   Understanding command syntax and shortcuts

7. **Installing Development Tools**

   o   Setting up popular programming languages (Python, Java, C++)

   o   Overview of package managers (APT, YUM, Snap, Flatpak)

   o   Configuring Git and other version control tools

8. **Connecting to the Internet and Networking**

- o Configuring Wi-Fi and Ethernet connections
- o Setting up SSH for remote server access
- o Using network diagnostic tools (ping, traceroute)

9. **Essential First Steps for Programmers**

- o Configuring a development-friendly text editor (Vim, VS Code)
- o Setting up an Integrated Development Environment (IDE)
- o Installing Docker or other container tools for development

10. **Using Linux in the Cloud**

- Introduction to running Linux on cloud platforms (AWS, Azure)
- Setting up a virtual private server (VPS)
- Real-world use cases: Deploying a simple web application

1.4 Real-World Applications of Linux

1. **Linux in Software Development**

- o Why major tech companies use Linux for development
- o Case studies of Linux in large-scale programming projects

2. **Linux for DevOps and Automation**

- o Integration with tools like Jenkins, Kubernetes, and Ansible
- o Practical examples of automating workflows with Linux

3. **Linux in Data Science and AI**
   - o Setting up Linux for Python-based data analysis
   - o How Linux supports GPU acceleration for AI training

4. **Linux in System Administration**
   - o Overview of server management and automation
   - o Examples of troubleshooting and maintaining a Linux-based system

---

1.5 *and Next Steps*

1. **Key Takeaways**
   - o Why Linux is essential for modern programming
   - o Benefits for developers beyond the basics

2. **What to Expect Next**
   - o Building a strong foundation with Linux commands (Chapter 2)
   - o Expanding into shell scripting and system administration

3. **Resources for Continued Learning**

- o Suggested reading materials and online tutorials
- o Engaging with the Linux community for hands-on experience

Chapter 2: Understanding Linux Distributions

2.1 Popular Linux Distributions: Ubuntu, CentOS, Debian, etc.

1. **What is a Linux Distribution?**
   - Explanation of how Linux distributions (distros) differ from the Linux kernel.
   - The role of distros in tailoring Linux for specific use cases.

2. **Overview of Major Linux Distributions**
   - **Ubuntu**:
     - Designed for ease of use; ideal for beginners and general-purpose users.
     - Broad software support and a large, active community.
     - Long-Term Support (LTS) releases for stability.
   - **Debian**:
     - A parent distribution for many others, including Ubuntu.
     - Focus on stability, open-source software, and a strong developer community.

- **CentOS** (and successors like Rocky Linux/AlmaLinux):
  - Known for enterprise-grade reliability.
  - Derived from Red Hat Enterprise Linux (RHEL); ideal for server environments.
- **Fedora**:
  - Cutting-edge software and a testing ground for RHEL.
  - Excellent for developers who want the latest technologies.
- **Arch Linux**:
  - Minimalistic and highly customizable; focuses on user control.
  - Requires technical expertise; popular among advanced users.
- **Mint**:
  - Built on Ubuntu and Debian; offers a Windows-like interface.
  - Great for users transitioning from other operating systems.
- **Kali Linux**:
  - Tailored for penetration testing and cybersecurity.
  - Comes with pre-installed tools for ethical hacking.

- o **Other Notable Distros**: SUSE Linux, Manjaro, Zorin OS, Elementary OS.

3. **Specialized Distributions**

- o Distros for embedded systems: Yocto Project, OpenWRT.
- o Lightweight distributions for older hardware: Puppy Linux, Tiny Core.
- o Cloud-optimized distros: CoreOS, RancherOS.

4. **Real-World Applications of Popular Distributions**

- o Examples of where and how these distros are used.
- o Case studies of companies leveraging specific distributions.

2.2 Choosing the Right Distribution for Programming

1. **Key Factors to Consider**

- o **Ease of Use**: Beginner-friendly distros like Ubuntu and Mint.
- o **Customization**: For advanced users who need full control, Arch or Gentoo.
- o **Stability vs. Cutting Edge**:
  - ▪ Stability: Debian, CentOS for long-term projects.

- Cutting Edge: Fedora, Arch for accessing the latest tools.
  - o **Community and Documentation**:
    - Importance of support and tutorials for troubleshooting.

2. **Programming Language Support**
   - o Distros optimized for specific languages or frameworks:
     - Python developers: Ubuntu, Debian (easy setup for data science tools).
     - Web developers: Fedora, Ubuntu (Docker and container support).
     - C++/C developers: Arch Linux (access to the latest compilers and libraries).

3. **Environment-Specific Recommendations**
   - o **For Personal Development**: Ubuntu, Fedora.
   - o **For Servers and Enterprise Use**: CentOS, RHEL, Debian.
   - o **For Experimentation and Learning**: Arch Linux, Fedora.

4. **Practical Tips for Making a Choice**
   - o Testing with live USBs or virtual machines before committing.
   - o Checking software and hardware compatibility.

2.3 Installation Guide

1. **Pre-Installation Preparations**
   - **Hardware Requirements**:
     - Minimum and recommended specifications for popular distros.
     - Ensuring compatibility with your machine's architecture (32-bit vs. 64-bit).
   - **Backing Up Data**:
     - Creating backups of important files before installation.
   - **Selecting Installation Media**:
     - Choosing between DVD, USB, or network installation.
     - Tools for creating bootable USBs: Rufus, Etcher, Balena.

2. **Step-by-Step Installation Process**
   - **Downloading ISO Images**:
     - Where to download reliable and official ISO files.
   - **Booting into the Installer**:
     - Accessing the boot menu and troubleshooting boot issues.
   - **Partitioning Your Disk**:
     - Guided vs. manual partitioning options.
     - Understanding partitions: /, /home, /swap.

- **Configuring System Settings**:
  - Choosing a time zone, keyboard layout, and default user settings.
- **Installing the Base System**:
  - What happens during the installation process.
- **Finalizing Installation**:
  - Post-installation updates and drivers.
  - Configuring the GRUB bootloader.

3. **Dual-Boot Installation**
  - **Setting Up Dual-Boot with Windows or macOS**:
    - Creating space for Linux alongside existing operating systems.
    - Configuring the bootloader to allow system selection at startup.

4. **Installing Linux in Virtual Machines**
  - Guide for using tools like VirtualBox, VMware, or QEMU.
  - Advantages of virtualization for beginners.

5. **Post-Installation Configuration**
  - **System Updates and Package Management**:
    - Using package managers (APT for Ubuntu/Debian, YUM/DNF for CentOS/Fedora).
  - **Installing Essential Tools for Programming**:

- Development environments, compilers, and IDEs.
  - **Customizing the Desktop Environment**:
    - Adjusting themes, settings, and desktop preferences.

6. **Troubleshooting Common Installation Issues**
   - Solutions for errors during installation or booting.
   - Where to seek help: Forums, official documentation, and community channels.

2.4 *and Practical Exercises*

1. **Key Takeaways**
   - Importance of choosing the right Linux distribution.
   - How to install and configure Linux for programming needs.

2. **Hands-On Exercises**
   - Test multiple distributions using live USBs.
   - Install Linux in a virtual machine and set up a simple programming environment.
   - Dual-boot a system with Linux and explore partitioning.

3. **Resources for Further Exploration**

o Recommended websites and forums for Linux beginners.

o Official documentation and guides for popular distributions.

Chapter 3: Navigating the Linux File System

3.1 Linux File System Hierarchy Explained

1. **Overview of the Linux File System**
   - Explanation of how Linux organizes data into a hierarchical structure starting with the root (/).
   - Differences from file systems on Windows and macOS.

2. **The Root Directory (/)**
   - Description of the root as the starting point of all directories.
   - Role of the root user in managing the file system.

3. **Hierarchical Structure of the File System**
   - Explanation of how directories branch out from the root.
   - Use of symbolic paths: absolute (/home/user) vs. relative (../user).

4. **The Filesystem Hierarchy Standard (FHS)**
   - Overview of FHS and its importance in maintaining consistency across distributions.
   - How FHS ensures developers and administrators can navigate any Linux system.

3.2 Essential Directories and Their Roles

1. **Key Directories in the Linux File System**
   - **/bin**: Essential user binaries (e.g., ls, cat, mkdir).
   - **/sbin**: System binaries for administrative tasks (e.g., iptables, reboot).
   - **/etc**: Configuration files for the system and applications.
   - **/home**: User home directories for personal files and configurations.
   - **/var**: Variable data such as logs, caches, and temporary files.
   - **/usr**: Secondary hierarchy for user applications and libraries.
   - **/lib and /lib64**: Essential shared libraries for binaries.
   - **/opt**: Optional software and third-party applications.
   - **/tmp**: Temporary files, cleared on reboot.
   - **/dev**: Device files for hardware like drives and peripherals.
   - **/mnt and /media**: Mount points for external and removable devices.
   - **/proc**: Virtual filesystem providing process and kernel information.
   - **/boot**: Files related to the bootloader and kernel.

2. **Practical Examples**

    o   Locating   configuration   files   in   /etc   (e.g.,
        etc/network/interfaces).

    o   Viewing system logs in /var/log.

    o   Accessing personal settings in /home/username.

3. **Directory Permissions**

    o   Explaining why some directories require root
        privileges.

    o   Navigating system directories safely as a regular user.

3.3 File Types and Their Purpose

1. **Understanding File Types in Linux**

    o   **Regular Files**: Text files, binaries, documents (- in ls
        output).

    o   **Directories**:   Containers   for   files   and   other
        directories (d in ls output).

    o   **Symbolic Links**: Pointers to other files (l in ls output).

    o   **Device Files**: Represent hardware devices (e.g.,
        /dev/sda, /dev/tty).

    o   **Sockets**: Inter-process communication endpoints.

    o   **Pipes**: Allow data transfer between processes.

2. **Viewing File Types**

    o   Using ls -l and file commands to identify file types.

- o Practical examples of symbolic links (ln -s source target).

3. **Special System Files**
   - o Hidden files starting with . (e.g., .bashrc, .profile).
   - o Configuration and metadata files in user directories.

3.4 File Permissions: Understanding and Managing Access

1. **Linux Permission Model**
   - o Explanation of ownership: user, group, and others.
   - o Permissions: Read (r), Write (w), and Execute (x).
   - o Default file permissions and the role of the umask.

2. **Interpreting File Permissions**
   - o Understanding the output of ls -l: Example: -rw-r--r-- 1 user group 4096 Jan 1 file.txt
     - First character: File type (-, d, l, etc.).
     - Next nine characters: Permissions for user, group, and others.
   - o How ownership impacts permissions.

3. **Modifying Permissions**
   - o Using chmod to change permissions:
     - Symbolic method: chmod u+x file.sh
     - Octal method: chmod 755 file.sh
   - o Practical examples:

- Granting execute permissions to a script.
- Restricting access to sensitive files.

4. **Changing Ownership**
   - Using chown to change file ownership:
     - Example: chown username:groupname file.txt.
   - Real-world scenario: Transferring ownership of project files.

5. **Understanding Special Permissions**
   - **SetUID and SetGID**: Running files with elevated permissions.
   - **Sticky Bit**: Preventing deletion of shared files by unauthorized users.

3.5 Real-World Applications and Best Practices

1. **Practical Use Cases for File Permissions**
   - Securing configuration files in /etc.
   - Managing collaborative projects in shared directories.

2. **Navigating and Managing the File System Efficiently**
   - Combining commands for power usage (find, grep, chmod).
   - Automating permission changes with scripts.

3. **Common Pitfalls to Avoid**
   - Overusing root permissions (sudo).

    o   Incorrect permission settings leading to security risks.

3.6 and Practical Exercises

1. **Key Takeaways**
   - o   The hierarchical structure of the Linux file system.
   - o   Roles of essential directories and how to use them.
   - o   Understanding and managing file permissions effectively.

2. **Hands-On Exercises**
   - o   Navigate the file system using cd, ls, and pwd.
   - o   Identify file types and permissions using ls -l and file.
   - o   Change permissions and ownership on sample files using chmod and chown.

3. **Resources for Further Exploration**
   - o   Official documentation on the Filesystem Hierarchy Standard (FHS).
   - o   Online tutorials for mastering Linux permissions.

Chapter 4: Basic Linux Commands

This chapter introduces essential Linux commands for navigating and managing files, working with text files, and searching or filtering data. These skills form the foundation for more advanced Linux tasks.

4.1 Command-Line Basics: Navigating and Managing Files

1. **Introduction to the Linux Shell**
   - Definition and role of the shell in Linux.
   - Common shells: Bash, Zsh, and Fish.
   - Opening the terminal and interacting with the command line.

2. **Navigation Commands**
   - **pwd**: Displaying the current directory path.
     - Example: Run pwd to find your location in the file system.
   - **ls**: Listing files and directories.
     - Options: ls -a (show hidden files), ls -l (detailed view).
   - **cd**: Changing directories.
     - Absolute paths: cd /home/user/documents.
     - Relative paths: cd ../ (move up one directory).

3. **File Management Commands**

- o **touch**: Creating empty files.
  - Example: touch file.txt to create a new file.
- o **mkdir**: Creating directories.
  - Example: mkdir projects to create a new folder.
- o **cp**: Copying files and directories.
  - Example: cp file1.txt file2.txt to duplicate a file.
- o **mv**: Moving or renaming files.
  - Example: mv oldname.txt newname.txt to rename a file.
- o **rm**: Removing files and directories.
  - Example: rm file.txt to delete a file.
  - Safety tip: Use rm -i for interactive deletion.
- o **rmdir**: Removing empty directories.

4. **Viewing and Managing File Sizes**

- o **du**: Checking disk usage of directories.
  - Example: du -h /home (human-readable format).
- o **df**: Displaying free disk space.
  - Example: df -h to view available and used disk space.

5. **Combining Commands with Pipes and Redirection**

- o **Pipes (|)**: Pass output from one command to another.
  - Example: ls -l | grep txt to list only .txt files.
- o **Redirection (>, >>)**: Save command output to files.
  - Example: ls > filelist.txt to save the list of files.

4.2 *Working with Text Files Using* cat, less, *and* nano

1. **Viewing Text Files**

   o **cat**: Concatenate and display text files.

      ▪ Example: cat file.txt to display the file's content.

      ▪ Use cat file1.txt file2.txt > combined.txt to merge files.

   o **less**: View large files one screen at a time.

      ▪ Navigation: Spacebar (next page), b (previous page), q (quit).

      ▪ Example: less log.txt for reading logs interactively.

2. **Editing Text Files**

   o **nano**: A simple text editor.

      ▪ Basic commands: Save (Ctrl+O), Exit (Ctrl+X), Search (Ctrl+W).

      ▪ Example: nano file.txt to open and edit a file.

3. **Real-World Use Cases**

   o Viewing system logs in /var/log.

   o Editing configuration files (e.g., /etc/network/interfaces).

4. **Additional Tools for Working with Text**

   o **head**: View the first lines of a file.

      ▪ Example: head -n 5 file.txt to see the first 5 lines.

- **tail**: View the last lines of a file.
  - Example: tail -f log.txt to monitor live updates in a log file.

4.3 Searching and Filtering with grep and find

1. **Searching Within Files Using grep**
   - Syntax: grep [options] pattern [file].
   - Examples:
     - grep "error" logfile.txt: Search for "error" in a log file.
     - grep -i "Warning" logfile.txt: Case-insensitive search.
     - grep -r "TODO" /home/user/projects: Recursive search across directories.

2. **Filtering and Customizing Output**
   - Highlight matches with --color option.
   - Combine grep with other commands:
     - Example: ls -l | grep "2025" to filter files modified in 2025.

3. **Finding Files and Directories Using find**
   - Syntax: find [path] [expression].
   - Examples:

- find /home -name "*.txt": Search for .txt files in /home.
- find /var -type d: Locate directories in /var.
- find . -size +1M: Find files larger than 1 MB.

4. **Combining find with Actions**
   o Deleting files: find /tmp -name "*.tmp" -delete.
   o Executing commands: find . -name "*.sh" -exec chmod +x {} \;.

5. **Real-World Applications**
   o Searching for error messages in logs.
   o Locating forgotten files or scripts in a project directory.
   o Automating clean-up tasks with find and scripts.

4.4 *and Practical Exercises*

1. **Key Takeaways**
   o Command-line navigation and file management are essential for productivity.
   o Tools like cat, less, and nano make working with text files simple.
   o Searching and filtering with grep and find saves time when handling large amounts of data.

2. **Hands-On Exercises**

- o   Use ls, cd, and pwd to explore your file system.
- o   Create a text file with nano, view it with cat, and append to it with >>.
- o   Use grep to search for a specific term in a log file.
- o   Find all .sh files in a directory and make them executable using find and chmod.

3. **Resources for Further Learning**

- o   Linux man pages: Run man [command] for detailed help.
- o   Online tutorials and cheat sheets for basic commands.

This chapter ensures readers gain a practical understanding of essential Linux commands, building their confidence to navigate, manage, and search files efficiently

Chapter 5: Managing Users and Groups

This chapter provides a comprehensive guide to managing users and groups in Linux, covering user creation, modification, deletion, group management, and the importance of sudo privileges. Real-world examples are included to demonstrate practical applications.

5.1 Creating, Modifying, and Deleting Users

1. **Understanding User Accounts in Linux**
   - o   Explanation of user accounts and their roles.
   - o   Difference between regular users and system users.
   - o   User data storage in /etc/passwd.

2. **Creating New Users**
   - o   **Using useradd:**
     - ▪   Syntax: useradd [options] username.
     - ▪   Example: useradd john creates a user named "john".
     - ▪   Options:
       - ▪   -m: Create a home directory.
       - ▪   -s: Specify the shell (e.g., -s /bin/bash).
     - ▪   Example: useradd -m -s /bin/bash john.
   - o   **Using adduser** (Debian-based systems):
     - ▪   Example: adduser john (interactive user creation).

- Includes prompts for password, home directory, and shell.

3. **Modifying Existing Users**
   - **Changing User Details**:
     - Command: usermod.
     - Example: usermod -s /bin/zsh john to change the shell.
     - Example: usermod -c "John Doe" john to update the user comment.
   - **Locking/Unlocking Accounts**:
     - Lock: usermod -L john.
     - Unlock: usermod -U john.

4. **Deleting Users**
   - **Using userdel**:
     - Command: userdel [options] username.
     - Example: userdel john removes the user.
     - Option: -r to delete the user's home directory.
   - Precautions before deleting a user account (e.g., backing up data).

5. **Real-World Scenarios**
   - Adding a new developer to a team with proper access rights.
   - Temporarily locking an account for security purposes.

5.2 User Permissions and Group Management

1. **Understanding User Permissions**
   - Ownership model: User, group, and others.
   - Permissions: Read (r), Write (w), and Execute (x).
   - Viewing permissions with ls -l.

2. **Groups in Linux**
   - Purpose of groups for managing user access.
   - Types of groups:
     - **Primary Group**: Assigned at user creation.
     - **Supplementary Groups**: Additional groups for extended permissions.

3. **Managing Groups**
   - **Creating Groups**:
     - Command: groupadd groupname.
     - Example: groupadd developers.
   - **Adding Users to Groups**:
     - Command: usermod -aG groupname username.
     - Example: usermod -aG developers john adds "john" to the "developers" group.
   - **Viewing Group Membership**:
     - Command: groups username.
     - Example: groups john.
   - **Changing Primary Group**:
     - Command: usermod -g groupname username.
     - Example: usermod -g developers john.

4. **Managing Permissions with Groups**

   o Assigning group ownership to files:

      ▪ Command: chgrp groupname filename.

      ▪ Example: chgrp developers project.txt.

   o Modifying group permissions with chmod.

5. **Real-World Applications**

   o Setting up group permissions for project collaboration.

   o Granting or restricting access to shared directories.

5.3 Sudo Privileges

1. **What is Sudo?**

   o Definition of sudo as a mechanism to execute commands with elevated privileges.

   o Importance of sudo over direct root access for security.

2. **Granting Sudo Privileges**

   o Adding a user to the sudo group:

      ▪ Command: usermod -aG sudo username (Debian-based).

      ▪ Example: usermod -aG sudo john.

   o Editing the sudoers file with visudo:

      ▪ Command: sudo visudo.

- Syntax: username ALL=(ALL) ALL.
  o Granting limited sudo access:
    - Example: Restricting "john" to use only specific commands.

3. **Best Practices for Sudo Usage**
   o Avoiding unnecessary sudo access for security.
   o Logging sudo activities to track changes.

4. **Real-World Scenarios**
   o Granting temporary sudo privileges to a contractor.
   o Using sudo to manage software installations securely.

5.4 Practical Examples and Exercises

1. **Examples**
   o Adding a new user with a home directory and assigning sudo privileges.
   o Creating a "developers" group and assigning access to a shared directory.
   o Revoking a user's access by removing them from a group.

2. **Hands-On Exercises**
   o Create a new user with the useradd or adduser command.
   o Add a user to multiple groups and verify membership.

- o Restrict permissions for a directory to a specific group using chmod and chgrp.
- o Experiment with sudo by installing a package (sudo apt install tree).

3. **Common Troubleshooting**

- o Resolving "permission denied" errors by adjusting group membership.
- o Fixing sudo access issues by editing the sudoers file.

5.5

1. **Key Takeaways**

- o Linux's robust user and group management system provides fine-grained control over permissions.
- o Groups simplify permission handling for multiple users.
- o Sudo is a powerful tool for managing administrative tasks securely.

2. **Next Steps**

- o Explore advanced group configurations.
- o Practice using sudo with different access restrictions.
- o Prepare for system administration by automating user and group tasks with scripts.

This chapter builds foundational skills for managing users, groups, and permissions, which are essential for system administration and collaborative environments

Chapter 6: Mastering File and Directory Permissions

This chapter dives into Linux file and directory permissions, covering essential tools like chmod, chown, and umask, with real-world scenarios and practical tips for securing files effectively.

6.1 Understanding chmod, chown, and umask

1. **Linux Permission Model**
   - Ownership categories:
     - **User (u)**: The owner of the file.
     - **Group (g)**: The group associated with the file.
     - **Others (o)**: All other users on the system.
   - Permission types:
     - **Read (r)**: Allows viewing file content.
     - **Write (w)**: Allows modifying file content.
     - **Execute (x)**: Allows running a file as a program or accessing a directory.

2. **Changing Permissions with chmod**
   - **Symbolic Method**:
     - Syntax: chmod [who][operator][permission] file.
     - Example: chmod u+x script.sh (add execute permission for the owner).

- Operators: + (add), - (remove), = (set explicitly).
  - o **Octal Method**:
    - Syntax: chmod [mode] file.
    - Understanding octal values:
      - 4: Read (r).
      - 2: Write (w).
      - 1: Execute (x).
      - Example: chmod 755 file.sh (owner: all permissions, group/others: read and execute).

3. **Changing Ownership with chown**
   - o **Basic Usage**:
     - Syntax: chown [owner][:group] file.
     - Example: chown alice file.txt (change owner to "alice").
     - Change owner and group: chown alice:developers file.txt.
   - o **Recursive Option**:
     - Example: chown -R alice /projects (apply changes to all files in /projects).

4. **Understanding and Configuring umask**
   - o **What is umask?**
     - Default permission mask applied when creating new files/directories.

- o **Viewing and Setting umask**:
  - Command: umask.
  - Example: umask 022 (default for most systems; prevents write access for group/others).
- o **Calculating Default Permissions**:
  - Formula: default permissions - umask.
  - Example: For files (666 - 022 = 644), for directories (777 - 022 = 755).

6.2 Real-World Scenarios of Permission Settings

1. **Collaboration on Projects**
   - o Shared directory for a team:
     - Example: /projects directory for the "developers" group.
     - Command:
       - chmod 770 /projects (full access for owner and group, no access for others).
       - chown alice:developers /projects.

2. **Securing Sensitive Files**
   - o Restrict access to confidential files:
     - Example: chmod 600 secret.txt (only owner has read/write access).

- o Change ownership to a privileged user:
  - chown root secret.txt.

3. **Managing Public Access**
   - o Setting up public read-only files:
     - Example: chmod 644 public.doc (owner: read/write, others: read only).
   - o Directory with public read access:
     - Example: chmod 755 /public.

4. **Automating Permissions for New Files**
   - o Setting umask for a group:
     - Example: For a team that needs full access, set umask 007 (default: 770 for directories, 660 for files).

5. **Troubleshooting Permission Issues**
   - o Diagnosing "Permission Denied" errors:
     - Using ls -l to check file permissions and ownership.
     - Adjust permissions with chmod or chown as needed.

6.3 Securing Files Effectively

1. **Best Practices for File Security**
   - o **Principle of Least Privilege**:

- Only grant the permissions required for a task.

○ **Avoiding chmod 777**:

- Risks of allowing full access to all users.

○ **Use Sudo for Administrative Tasks**:

- Avoid logging in as root; use sudo for elevated privileges.

2. **Special Permissions**

○ **SetUID and SetGID**:

- Allow programs to execute with elevated privileges.

- Example: chmod u+s script.sh (set SetUID on a file).

○ **Sticky Bit**:

- Prevent unauthorized file deletion in shared directories.

- Example: chmod +t /shared.

3. **Using ACLs for Advanced Permissions**

○ **Access Control Lists (ACLs)**:

- Provide fine-grained permissions for multiple users or groups.

- Example: setfacl -m u:john:rwx file.txt (grant "john" full access to a file).

○ Viewing ACLs: getfacl file.txt.

4. **Encrypting Sensitive Data**

○ Tools for encrypting files:

- **GPG**:
  - Example: gpg -c secret.txt (encrypt secret.txt with a passphrase).
- File encryption in transit: Use scp or rsync over SSH.

5. **Monitoring and Auditing Permissions**
   - **Audit Logs**:
     - Enable auditing to track file access.
   - Using tools like find to identify misconfigured files:
     - Example: find / -perm 777 (list all files with 777 permissions).

6.4 Practical Examples and Exercises

1. **Examples**
   - Use chmod to set execute permissions for a script and run it.
   - Configure shared directory access for a team using chown and chmod.
   - Use umask to create a secure environment for new files.

2. **Hands-On Exercises**
   - Create a directory with read-only access for others.

- o Add a sticky bit to a shared directory and test its behavior.
- o Encrypt a file with GPG and verify access.

3. **Common Troubleshooting**
   - o Fixing incorrect ownership with chown.
   - o Resetting overly permissive files using chmod.

6.5

1. **Key Takeaways**
   - o Permissions (chmod), ownership (chown), and default masks (umask) are the foundation of Linux file security.
   - o Real-world permission management ensures secure collaboration and data protection.
   - o Special permissions and encryption add layers of security for critical files.

2. **Next Steps**
   - o Practice setting up secure file structures.
   - o Explore ACLs for advanced permission control.
   - o Prepare for system administration tasks by mastering these tools.

Chapter 7: Working with Processes and Jobs

This chapter explores how to view, manage, and control processes and jobs in Linux. It also covers automation using cron and at for scheduling tasks, ensuring readers gain a strong grasp of process and job management.

7.1 Viewing and Managing Processes with ps and top

1. **Understanding Linux Processes**
   - What is a process? Explanation of running programs and their life cycles.
   - Types of processes: Foreground, background, and system processes.
   - Parent and child processes: Overview of process trees.

2. **Using the ps Command**
   - **Basic Usage**:
     - ps displays running processes for the current shell session.
     - Example: ps lists your current session's active processes.
   - **Extended Information**:

- ps -e: View all processes on the system.
- ps aux: Detailed process information, including memory and CPU usage.
- Example: ps aux | grep apache to find processes related to Apache.
  - Customizing ps output:
    - Example: ps -eo pid,ppid,cmd,%mem,%cpu (display specific columns).

3. **Using the top Command**
   - **Overview**:
     - Interactive tool to monitor real-time system activity.
   - Key metrics:
     - CPU and memory usage.
     - Process priority (PR) and niceness (NI).
   - Navigating top:
     - q: Quit.
     - k: Kill a process by entering its PID.
     - r: Renice a process to adjust its priority.
   - Alternative tool: **htop** (a more user-friendly version of top).

4. **Managing Processes**
   - Killing a process:
     - Command: kill PID.

- Example: kill 1234 to terminate a process with PID 1234.
- Force-kill: kill -9 PID.
  o Viewing a process tree:
    - Command: pstree.
    - Example: pstree -p (shows PIDs).

7.2 Controlling Jobs: Background and Foreground Processes

1. **Foreground and Background Processes**
   o Running processes in the foreground:
     - Example: Running python script.py keeps it active in the terminal.
   o Sending a process to the background:
     - Command: command &.
     - Example: sleep 300 & runs a process in the background.
   o Viewing background jobs:
     - Command: jobs.
     - Example: [1]+ Running sleep 300 &.

2. **Controlling Background Jobs**
   o Suspending a process:
     - Shortcut: Ctrl+Z.
     - Example: Suspend ping google.com with Ctrl+Z.

- o Resuming a job in the background:
  - Command: bg %job_number.
  - Example: bg %1 resumes job 1 in the background.
- o Bringing a background job to the foreground:
  - Command: fg %job_number.
  - Example: fg %1 resumes job 1 in the foreground.

3. **Real-World Applications**

- o Running long scripts in the background while working on other tasks.
- o Managing suspended jobs during debugging or multitasking.

7.3 Automation with cron and at

1. **Overview of Task Automation**
   - o Importance of automating repetitive tasks.
   - o Difference between cron (recurring tasks) and at (one-time tasks).

2. **Using cron for Recurring Tasks**
   - o Setting up cron jobs:
     - Command: crontab -e to edit the cron table.
     - Syntax: minute hour day month weekday command.

- Example: 0 5 * * * /home/user/backup.sh (runs a backup script daily at 5:00 AM).
  - Viewing existing cron jobs:
    - Command: crontab -l.
  - Removing a cron job:
    - Command: crontab -r.
  - Real-world examples:
    - Scheduling log rotations.
    - Automating system updates.

3. **Using at for One-Time Tasks**
   - Setting up a one-time job:
     - Command: at [time].
     - Example: at 14:00 schedules a task for 2:00 PM.
   - Adding a command interactively:
     - Example: Type shutdown -h now, press Ctrl+D to save.
   - Viewing scheduled tasks:
     - Command: atq.
   - Removing tasks:
     - Command: atrm [job_number].

4. **Monitoring and Troubleshooting Automated Tasks**
   - Checking logs for cron:
     - Example: View /var/log/syslog or /var/log/cron.
   - Debugging cron jobs:

- Ensuring proper paths and permissions in scripts.
- Redirecting output to log files (e.g., command > logfile 2>&1).

7.4 Practical Examples and Exercises

1. **Examples**
   - Use ps to find and kill a process consuming excessive CPU.
   - Run a script in the background, suspend it, and resume it.
   - Create a cron job to automate backups.
   - Use at to schedule a one-time task, then cancel it.

2. **Hands-On Exercises**
   - Monitor system activity with top and identify the top CPU-consuming process.
   - Create a script that logs the date and time, then schedule it with cron.
   - Use jobs, fg, and bg to manage processes interactively.

3. **Common Troubleshooting**
   - Resolving "Permission Denied" issues by using sudo or checking file paths.
   - Diagnosing failed cron jobs by checking output logs.

7.5

1. **Key Takeaways**
   - o Tools like ps and top provide insights into system processes.
   - o Background and foreground job management allows multitasking effectively.
   - o Automation with cron and at enhances productivity by scheduling repetitive tasks.

2. **Next Steps**
   - o Explore advanced process management tools like systemd.
   - o Automate complex workflows using shell scripts combined with cron.

This chapter equips readers with practical skills for managing processes and jobs, ensuring they can monitor and control system activity while leveraging automation to streamline tasks.

Chapter 8: Networking Essentials for Programmers

This chapter introduces foundational networking concepts and tools essential for programmers. It covers network configuration, troubleshooting, common networking commands, and secure remote access with SSH.

8.1 Configuring and Troubleshooting Network Settings

1. **Understanding Networking Basics**
   - Overview of IP addresses, subnet masks, and gateways.
   - Difference between private and public IP addresses.
   - Importance of DNS in resolving domain names.

2. **Configuring Network Settings**
   - Viewing current network settings:
     - Command: ip addr or ifconfig (legacy).
     - Example: ip addr show to display IP addresses and network interfaces.
   - Assigning a static IP address:
     - Edit network configuration files (e.g., /etc/network/interfaces for Debian-based systems).

- Example configuration:

  plaintext

  iface eth0 inet static
  address 192.168.1.100
  netmask 255.255.255.0
  gateway 192.168.1.1

- o Restarting network services:
  - Command: systemctl restart networking or nmcli for NetworkManager.
- o Configuring DNS servers:
  - Edit /etc/resolv.conf to include nameserver entries.

3. **Troubleshooting Network Issues**
   - o Checking connectivity:
     - Command: ping.
     - Example: ping google.com to test internet connection.
   - o Diagnosing interface problems:
     - Use ip link or ifconfig to check interface status.
     - Enable an interface: ip link set eth0 up.
   - o Analyzing routing issues:
     - Command: ip route or route -n (legacy).
     - Adding a route: ip route add default via 192.168.1.1.
   - o Viewing active connections and ports:

- Command: netstat or ss (preferred).
- Example: ss -tuln to list open ports.

8.2 Networking Commands: ping, netstat, curl, and wget

1. **Using ping for Connectivity Testing**
   - Syntax: ping [hostname or IP].
   - Example: ping 8.8.8.8 to test connection to Google's DNS server.
   - Options:
     - -c: Limit the number of packets (e.g., ping -c 5 google.com).
     - -i: Set the interval between packets (e.g., ping -i 2 google.com).

2. **Using netstat (or ss) for Network Statistics**
   - Viewing active connections:
     - Example: netstat -tuln or ss -tuln (TCP/UDP listening ports).
   - Monitoring network statistics:
     - Example: netstat -s for protocol-specific statistics.
   - Finding processes using ports:
     - Command: netstat -p or ss -p.

3. **Using curl for HTTP Requests**

- o **Basic Syntax**:
  - curl [URL].
  - Example: curl https://example.com fetches a webpage's HTML content.
- o **Downloading Files**:
  - Example: curl -O https://example.com/file.zip.
- o **Sending Data**:
  - Example: curl -X POST -d "param=value" https://example.com/api.
- o Debugging network issues with curl:
  - Example: curl -I https://example.com fetches HTTP headers.

4. **Using wget for File Downloads**
   - o **Basic Syntax**:
     - wget [URL].
     - Example: wget https://example.com/file.zip.
   - o **Recursive Downloads**:
     - Example: wget -r https://example.com/docs/ downloads an entire directory structure.
   - o Handling download interruptions:
     - Example: wget -c https://example.com/file.zip resumes an interrupted download.

8.3 Introduction to SSH and Remote Access

1. **What is SSH?**

   o Explanation of Secure Shell (SSH) for encrypted remote access.

   o SSH architecture: Client-server model.

2. **Setting Up an SSH Server**

   o Installing the OpenSSH server:

     ▪ Command: sudo apt install openssh-server.

   o Starting and enabling the SSH service:

     ▪ Command: sudo systemctl start ssh and sudo systemctl enable ssh.

3. **Using SSH for Remote Access**

   o Syntax: ssh [user]@[hostname or IP].

   o Example: ssh alice@192.168.1.100 connects to a remote machine as user "alice".

   o Adding an SSH key for passwordless login:

     ▪ Generate a key pair: ssh-keygen.

     ▪ Copy the public key to the server: ssh-copy-id alice@192.168.1.100.

4. **Secure File Transfer Using SSH**

   o Using scp for file transfer:

     ▪ Syntax: scp [source] [destination].

     ▪ Example: scp file.txt alice@192.168.1.100:/home/alice/.

   o Using rsync for efficient file synchronization:

- Example: rsync -avz local_dir/ alice@192.168.1.100:/remote_dir/.

5. **Advanced SSH Features**

   o Port forwarding:

      - Syntax: ssh -L [local_port]:[remote_host]:[remote_port] user@server.

      - Example: ssh -L 8080:localhost:80 alice@192.168.1.100.

   o Using SSH tunnels for secure browsing.

8.4 Practical Examples and Exercises

1. **Examples**

   o Test connectivity to a server using ping.

   o Use curl to fetch data from a public API.

   o List open ports on your system with ss -tuln.

   o Transfer a file to a remote server using scp.

2. **Hands-On Exercises**

   o Configure a static IP address and verify connectivity.

   o Schedule a recurring download of a file using wget and cron.

   o Set up SSH key-based authentication for secure remote access.

3. **Common Troubleshooting**

- o Diagnosing "Connection Refused" errors:
  - Check firewall settings or ensure SSH service is running.
- o Resolving DNS issues by testing with an IP address.

8.5

1. **Key Takeaways**
   - o Network configuration and troubleshooting are critical skills for programmers.
   - o Commands like ping, netstat, curl, and wget help monitor and interact with network resources.
   - o SSH provides secure remote access and file transfer capabilities.

2. **Next Steps**
   - o Explore advanced SSH configurations for port forwarding and tunneling.
   - o Learn about firewalls and network security tools like iptables.

This chapter ensures a solid understanding of Linux networking essentials, empowering programmers to configure, troubleshoot, and interact with networks effectively.

Chapter 9: Package Management Systems

This chapter delves into Linux package management, focusing on popular package managers (APT, YUM, and DNF), software installation and updates, and troubleshooting dependency issues.

9.1 Understanding Package Managers: APT, YUM, and DNF

1. **What is a Package Manager?**

   o Definition: A tool for installing, upgrading, configuring, and removing software.

   o Role of package managers in maintaining system consistency.

2. **Package Management Concepts**

   o Repositories: Centralized locations for software packages.

   o Types of packages:

     ▪ **Binary Packages**: Precompiled software ready for installation.

     ▪ **Source Packages**: Software that must be compiled before use.

3. **Popular Package Managers**

   o **APT (Advanced Package Tool)**:

     ▪ Used by Debian-based distributions like Ubuntu.

- Commands: apt-get, apt, and dpkg.
  - **YUM (Yellowdog Updater, Modified)**:
    - Used by CentOS and older versions of Red Hat.
    - Now mostly replaced by DNF.
  - **DNF (Dandified YUM)**:
    - Modern replacement for YUM.
    - Used in Fedora, CentOS Stream, and Red Hat Enterprise Linux.

4. **Comparison of Package Managers**

   - Advantages of APT: Simplicity and large repository support.
   - Advantages of DNF: Better dependency handling and faster performance.
   - Choosing the right manager based on your distribution.

9.2 Installing, Updating, and Removing Software

1. **Installing Software**

   - **APT**:
     - Syntax: sudo apt install package-name.
     - Example: sudo apt install vim.
   - **YUM/ DNF**:

- Syntax: sudo yum install package-name or sudo dnf install package-name.
- Example: sudo dnf install nano.

2. Updating Software

- o **APT**:
  - Update package list: sudo apt update.
  - Upgrade installed packages: sudo apt upgrade.
  - Example: sudo apt update && sudo apt upgrade.

- o **YUM/ DNF**:
  - Update system: sudo yum update or sudo dnf update.
  - Example: sudo dnf update.

3. Removing Software

- o **APT**:
  - Syntax: sudo apt remove package-name.
  - Remove configuration files: sudo apt purge package-name.
  - Example: sudo apt remove apache2.

- o **YUM/ DNF**:
  - Syntax: sudo yum remove package-name or sudo dnf remove package-name.
  - Example: sudo dnf remove httpd.

4. Managing Individual Packages

- o Installing from .deb files with APT:
  - Example: sudo dpkg -i package.deb.

- Fix broken dependencies: sudo apt install -f.

o Installing from .rpm files with YUM/DNF:

- Example: sudo dnf install package.rpm.

9.3 Resolving Dependency Issues

1. **Understanding Dependencies**

   o Definition: Software components required for a package to function.

   o Importance of dependency resolution by package managers.

2. **Common Dependency Issues**

   o Broken dependencies due to missing or outdated packages.

   o Conflicts when multiple packages require different versions of the same dependency.

3. **Resolving Dependency Issues**

   o Using APT:

   - Fix dependencies: sudo apt --fix-broken install.

   - Check for missing dependencies: sudo apt install -f.

   o Using YUM/DNF:

   - Install missing dependencies: sudo yum install package-name or sudo dnf install package-name.

- Enable additional repositories:
  - Example: sudo dnf config-manager --add-repo repository_url.
- Force installation of specific versions:
  - Example: sudo apt install package-name=version.

4. **Best Practices for Managing Dependencies**

- Keep repositories updated with sudo apt update or sudo dnf makecache.
- Avoid using non-standard repositories unless necessary.
- Use virtual environments for language-specific packages (e.g., Python's venv).

9.4 Practical Examples and Exercises

1. **Examples**

- Install a text editor like nano using APT and DNF.
- Upgrade all installed packages on your system.
- Remove an unused package and clean up configuration files.

2. **Hands-On Exercises**

- Add a new repository and install software from it.
- Use sudo apt install -f to fix a broken package installation.

- o Resolve a dependency issue when installing a .deb or .rpm package.

3. **Common Troubleshooting**

- o Dealing with "Package Not Found" errors:
  - Ensure repositories are updated (sudo apt update or sudo dnf makecache).
- o Resolving "Dependency Hell":
  - Remove conflicting packages and retry installation.
- o Checking logs for more details:
  - APT: /var/log/apt/term.log.
  - DNF: /var/log/dnf.log.

9.5

1. **Key Takeaways**

- o Package managers like APT, YUM, and DNF simplify software installation and updates.
- o Resolving dependency issues ensures a stable and functional system.
- o Regular maintenance with updates and cleanup improves system reliability.

2. **Next Steps**

o Explore advanced package management tools like snap and flatpak.

o Learn to create and manage custom repositories.

Chapter 10: Linux Text Processing Tools

This chapter introduces powerful text processing tools in Linux, including awk, sed, and cut. It provides practical examples for scripts and demonstrates the use of regular expressions to manipulate and analyze text efficiently.

10.1 Tools Like awk, sed, and cut

1. **Overview of Text Processing in Linux**
   - Text processing involves manipulating text data from files, streams, or command outputs.
   - Importance for log analysis, data extraction, and scripting.

2. **awk: A Pattern Scanning and Processing Language**
   - **Basic Syntax**:
     - awk 'pattern {action}' file.
   - **Key Features**:
     - Field-based processing: $1, $2, etc., represent fields in a line.
     - Default behavior: Print lines matching a pattern.
   - **Examples**:
     - Print the first column of a file:

bash

awk '{print $1}' file.txt

- Find lines containing "error":

bash

awk '/error/' log.txt

- Calculate the sum of a column:

bash

awk '{sum += $2} END {print sum}' file.txt

3. **sed: A Stream Editor**

   o **Basic Syntax**:
   - sed 's/pattern/replacement/' file.

   o **Key Features**:
   - Perform inline text replacements.
   - Extract and delete text.

   o **Examples**:
   - Replace "foo" with "bar" in a file:

bash

sed 's/foo/bar/' file.txt

- Delete lines containing "temp":

  bash

  sed '/temp/d' file.txt

- Append text after a specific line:

  bash

  sed '/pattern/a\Text to append' file.txt

4. **cut: Extracting Specific Parts of Text**

   o **Basic Syntax**:

     - cut [options] file.

   o **Key Features**:

     - Extract columns, characters, or fields based on delimiters.

   o **Examples**:

     - Extract the first 10 characters from each line:

       bash

       cut -c1-10 file.txt

     - Extract the third field from a CSV file:

       bash

```
cut -d',' -f3 file.csv
```

10.2 Practical Examples of Text Processing for Scripts

1. **Filtering Logs**
   - Extracting error messages:

   bash

   ```
   grep 'ERROR' /var/log/syslog | cut -d' ' -f5-
   ```

   - Highlighting failed login attempts:

   bash

   ```
   awk '/Failed/ {print $0}' auth.log
   ```

2. **Manipulating CSV Data**
   - Calculate the total of a specific column:

   bash

   ```
   awk -F',' '{sum += $3} END {print sum}' data.csv
   ```

   - Replace a field value:

   bash

   ```
   sed 's/old_value/new_value/' file.csv
   ```

3. **Automating File Cleanup**

   o Removing temporary or backup files:

   bash

   find . -name '*.tmp' -exec sed -i '/temp/d' {} \;

4. **Combining Tools for Advanced Processing**

   o Extract and sort unique IP addresses from logs:

   bash

   awk '{print $1}' access.log | sort | uniq

10.3 Regular Expressions in Linux

1. **What Are Regular Expressions?**

   o Patterns used to match, search, and manipulate text.

   o Types of regular expressions in Linux:

      ▪ **Basic Regular Expressions (BRE)**: Used in tools like grep.

      ▪ **Extended Regular Expressions (ERE)**: Used in tools like awk and sed.

2. **Regular Expression Syntax**

   o **Characters and Operators**:

      ▪ .: Matches any single character.

- *: Matches zero or more of the preceding character.
- ^: Matches the start of a line.
- $: Matches the end of a line.
- []: Matches any character inside the brackets.

○ **Examples**:

- Match lines starting with "ERROR":

bash

grep '^ERROR' file.txt

- Find email addresses:

bash

grep -E '[a-zA-Z0-9._%+-]+@[a-zA-Z0-9.-]+\.[a-zA-Z]{2,}' file.txt

- Replace all digits with "X":

bash

sed 's/[0-9]/X/g' file.txt

3. **Using Regular Expressions with Tools**

○ **grep**:

- Search for lines containing "user123":

bash

grep 'user123' file.txt

- o **awk:**
  - Print lines where the second field matches a pattern:

    bash

    awk '$2 ~ /pattern/' file.txt

- o **sed:**
  - Delete all lines matching a pattern:

    bash

    sed '/pattern/d' file.txt

10.4 Practical Examples and Exercises

1. **Examples**
   - o Use awk to extract specific columns from a space-delimited file.
   - o Use sed to replace all occurrences of "foo" with "bar" in a file.
   - o Extract usernames from a system log with cut.
2. **Hands-On Exercises**

- o Write a script to process a log file, extracting errors and saving them to a new file.
- o Use awk to calculate averages from numeric data in a CSV file.
- o Apply regular expressions with grep to find and count lines matching a pattern.

3. **Common Troubleshooting**

- o Debugging regular expressions by testing patterns with grep.
- o Resolving unexpected results from awk or sed due to incorrect delimiters.

10.5

1. **Key Takeaways**

- o Tools like awk, sed, and cut simplify text manipulation.
- o Regular expressions add powerful pattern-matching capabilities.
- o Practical examples demonstrate the real-world value of text processing.

2. **Next Steps**

- o Explore advanced text processing with Python or Perl.

- o Integrate text processing into shell scripts for automation.

This chapter ensures readers gain confidence using Linux text processing tools, enabling efficient data manipulation and script writing.

Chapter 11: Introduction to Shell Scripting

This chapter introduces the basics of Bash scripting, walks through the process of writing your first shell script, and provides best practices for creating efficient and maintainable scripts.

11.1 Basics of Bash Scripting

1. **What is Shell Scripting?**
   - A shell script is a program written for the shell to automate tasks.
   - Benefits of shell scripting:
     - Automates repetitive tasks.
     - Simplifies complex workflows.
     - Enhances productivity for system administration and programming.

2. **Understanding the Bash Shell**
   - Bash (Bourne Again Shell) is the most widely used shell in Linux.
   - Key features of Bash:
     - Variables, conditionals, loops, and functions.
     - Command substitution and piping.

3. **Essential Components of a Shell Script**

- o **Shebang (#!)**:
  - The first line of a script specifies the interpreter.
  - Example: #!/bin/bash.
- o **Commands**:
  - Basic Linux commands like ls, echo, grep.
- o **Variables**:
  - Syntax: VAR_NAME=value.
  - Access: $VAR_NAME.
  - Example:

  bash

  NAME="John"
  echo "Hello, $NAME"

- o **Comments**:
  - Use # to add comments for documentation.
  - Example:

  bash

  # This is a comment

4. **Permissions and Execution**
   - o Make a script executable:
     - Command: chmod +x script.sh.
   - o Run a script:

- Syntax: ./script.sh.

11.2 Writing Your First Shell Script

1. **Creating a Simple Script**

   o Example: "Hello, World!" script.

   bash

   ```bash
   #!/bin/bash
   echo "Hello, World!"
   ```

   o Steps:

      1. Open a text editor (e.g., nano or vim).
      2. Write the script.
      3. Save the file (e.g., hello.sh).
      4. Make it executable: chmod +x hello.sh.
      5. Execute: ./hello.sh.

2. **Working with Variables**

   o Example: Greet a user with their name.

   bash

   ```bash
   #!/bin/bash
   NAME="Alice"
   echo "Hello, $NAME!"
   ```

3. Using Command-Line Arguments

o Access arguments with $1, $2, etc.

o Example: Greet a user provided as an argument.

bash

```
#!/bin/bash
echo "Hello, $1!"
```

4. Adding Conditionals

o Example: Check if a file exists.

bash

```
#!/bin/bash
if [ -f "$1" ]; then
  echo "File $1 exists."
else
  echo "File $1 does not exist."
fi
```

5. Implementing Loops

o Example: Print numbers 1 to 5.

bash

```
#!/bin/bash
for i in {1..5}; do
  echo "Number: $i"
done
```

11.3 Best Practices for Shell Scripting

1. **Write Clean and Readable Code**

   o   Use meaningful variable names.

   o   Add comments to explain the script's logic.

2. **Error Handling**

   o   Check for errors and handle them gracefully.

   o   Example: Use if conditions to verify input arguments.

   bash

   ```bash
   if [ "$#" -ne 1 ]; then
     echo "Usage: $0 filename"
     exit 1
   fi
   ```

3. **Follow a Consistent Style**

   o   Indent nested blocks.

   o   Use spaces around operators.

4. **Use Built-In Commands and Utilities**

   o   Prefer built-in commands like test, echo, and printf for compatibility.

   o   Avoid unnecessary external commands.

5. **Make Scripts Modular**

   o   Break complex scripts into smaller functions.

   o   Example:

bash

```
greet_user() {
  echo "Hello, $1!"
}
greet_user "Alice"
```

6. Handle Permissions Carefully

- o Avoid running scripts as root unless necessary.
- o Test scripts on non-critical systems before deploying them.

7. Use Debugging Tools

- o Enable debugging with set -x.
- o Run the script: bash -x script.sh.

8. Ensure Cross-Platform Compatibility

- o Avoid features specific to a single shell or system.

11.4 Practical Examples and Exercises

1. Examples

- o Create a script to back up a directory:

bash

```
#!/bin/bash
tar -czf backup.tar.gz $1
echo "Backup of $1 completed."
```

- o Write a script to monitor disk usage:

bash

```
#!/bin/bash
df -h | grep '/dev/sda1'
```

2. Hands-On Exercises

- o Write a script to list all files in a directory.
- o Create a script that accepts a username and greets them.
- o Write a script to calculate the factorial of a number using a loop.

3. Common Troubleshooting

- o Verify correct permissions if the script doesn't execute.
- o Check for syntax errors by running bash script.sh.

11.5

1. Key Takeaways

- o Shell scripting is a powerful tool for automating tasks.
- o A solid foundation in Bash scripting enables more efficient workflows.
- o Best practices ensure scripts are reliable, maintainable, and secure.

2. **Next Steps**

   o Explore advanced scripting topics like arrays, trap commands, and debugging.

   o Practice integrating shell scripts into real-world workflows.

This chapter lays a strong foundation for shell scripting, enabling readers to create efficient scripts for automation and problem-solving.

Chapter 12: Advanced Shell Scripting Techniques

This chapter delves deeper into shell scripting with advanced concepts, including loops, conditionals, functions, debugging techniques, optimization strategies, and real-world automation examples.

12.1 Using Loops, Conditionals, and Functions

1. **Loops in Shell Scripting**
   - **For Loop**:
     - Iterate over a sequence or list.
     - Example: Print all files in a directory.

       bash

       ```
       for file in /path/to/directory/*; do
         echo "File: $file"
       done
       ```

   - **While Loop**:
     - Execute commands as long as a condition is true.
     - Example: Count down from 5 to 1.

bash

```
count=5
while [ $count -gt 0 ]; do
  echo "Count: $count"
  ((count--))
done
```

- o **Until Loop**:
  - Execute commands until a condition becomes true.
  - Example: Wait for a file to exist.

  bash

  ```
  until [ -f "file.txt" ]; do
    echo "Waiting for file.txt..."
    sleep 1
  done
  ```

2. **Advanced Conditionals**
   - o **Nested Conditionals**:
     - Example: Check multiple conditions.

     bash

     ```
     if [ -d "/backup" ]; then
       echo "Backup directory exists."
     elif [ -f "/backup.tar.gz" ]; then
       echo "Backup file exists."
     ```

```
else
  echo "No backup found."
fi
```

- o **Case Statement**:
  - Cleaner alternative to if-elif for multiple conditions.
  - Example: Handle user input.

  bash

```
read -p "Enter a choice (start/stop): " choice
case $choice in
  start) echo "Starting service...";;
  stop) echo "Stopping service...";;
  *) echo "Invalid choice!";;
esac
```

3. **Functions in Shell Scripts**
   - o **Defining and Using Functions**:
     - Example: A reusable function for logging messages.

     bash

```
log_message() {
  echo "$(date): $1"
}
log_message "Script started."
```

- ○ **Passing Arguments to Functions**:
  - ▪ Example: Calculate the sum of two numbers.

    bash

    ```
    calculate_sum() {
      echo "Sum: $(($1 + $2))"
    }
    calculate_sum 10 20
    ```

- ○ **Return Values from Functions**:
  - ▪ Example: Check if a number is even or odd.

    bash

    ```
    is_even() {
      return $(($1 % 2))
    }
    is_even 4 && echo "Even" || echo "Odd"
    ```

12.2 Debugging and Optimizing Scripts

1. **Debugging Techniques**
   - ○ Enable debugging with set -x:
     - ▪ Add set -x at the top of the script to trace command execution.
     - ▪ Example:

```
bash


set -x
echo "Debugging enabled"
```

- o Run the script in debug mode:
    - Command: bash -x script.sh.
- o Use set -e to stop execution on errors.

2. **Error Handling**

- o **Trap Command**:
    - Catch errors and signals.
    - Example: Cleanup on script interruption.

```
bash


trap 'echo "Script interrupted! Cleaning up..."; rm -f temp.txt' INT
```

- o Check command success with $?:
    - Example:

```
bash


if ! command; then
  echo "Command failed."
fi
```

3. **Optimization Strategies**

- o Avoid unnecessary external commands:

- Replace expr with $((...)) for arithmetic.
- Replace cat with redirection (<).
  o Use built-in features:
    - Example: Use arrays for complex data structures.

bash

```
arr=("one" "two" "three")
for val in "${arr[@]}"; do
  echo $val
done
```

12.3 Real-World Automation Scripts

1. **Backup Script**
   o Automate directory backups with timestamps.

bash

```
#!/bin/bash
src="/path/to/source"
dest="/path/to/backup"
backup_name="backup_$(date +%Y%m%d).tar.gz"

tar -czf "$dest/$backup_name" "$src"
echo "Backup created: $dest/$backup_name"
```

2. **System Monitoring Script**

o Monitor disk usage and send an alert if usage exceeds 90%.

bash

```
#!/bin/bash
threshold=90
usage=$(df / | grep / | awk '{print $5}' | sed 's/%//')

if [ $usage -gt $threshold ]; then
  echo "Disk usage is above $threshold%! Current usage: $usage%"
fi
```

3. **Log Rotation Script**

o Archive old logs and delete logs older than 7 days.

bash

```
#!/bin/bash
log_dir="/var/log/myapp"
archive_dir="/var/log/myapp/archive"

mkdir -p $archive_dir
find $log_dir -name "*.log" -mtime +7 -exec mv {} $archive_dir \;
tar -czf $archive_dir/logs_$(date +%Y%m%d).tar.gz $archive_dir/*.log
find $archive_dir -name "*.log" -delete
echo "Logs rotated and archived."
```

4. Automation with APIs

o Fetch data from a REST API and save it to a file.

bash

```
#!/bin/bash
api_url="https://api.example.com/data"
output_file="data.json"

curl -s $api_url -o $output_file
echo "Data fetched and saved to $output_file."
```

12.4 Practical Examples and Exercises

1. Examples

o Write a script to compress all .txt files in a directory.

o Create a function to check if a given IP address is reachable using ping.

o Implement error handling to clean up temporary files on failure.

2. Hands-On Exercises

o Automate a task to send an email alert when CPU usage exceeds 80%.

o Write a script to download and organize daily reports from an FTP server.

o Debug and optimize an existing script to improve its performance.

3. **Common Troubleshooting**

- o Fix infinite loops by adding proper exit conditions.
- o Debug unexpected behavior with strategic echo statements.
- o Check for syntax errors using bash -n script.sh.

12.5

1. **Key Takeaways**

- o Advanced features like loops, conditionals, and functions make scripts powerful and reusable.
- o Debugging and optimization ensure reliability and efficiency.
- o Real-world automation scripts save time and reduce errors.

2. **Next Steps**

- o Explore more complex topics like input validation, parallel processing, and using external libraries.
- o Combine shell scripting with other programming languages like Python for hybrid workflows.

This chapter equips readers with advanced scripting techniques, empowering them to create robust, efficient, and practical automation solutions.

Chapter 13: Version Control with Git

This chapter introduces Git, a powerful version control system widely used in software development. It covers setting up Git on Linux, performing basic Git operations, and integrating Git into your development workflow.

13.1 Setting Up Git on Linux

1. **Installing Git**

    o   Check if Git is already installed:

    ▪   Command: git --version.

    o   Install Git on popular distributions:

    ▪   **Debian/Ubuntu**:

    bash

    sudo apt update
    sudo apt install git

    ▪   **CentOS/RHEL**:

    bash

    sudo yum install git

    ▪   **Fedora**:

bash

sudo dnf install git

2. **Configuring Git**

   o   Set up your name and email:

   bash

   git config --global user.name "Your Name"
   git config --global user.email "your.email@example.com"

   o   Verify configuration:

   bash

   git config --list

3. **Understanding the Git Directory Structure**

   o   **Working Directory**: Your project folder.

   o   **Staging Area**: A space where changes are prepared for a commit.

   o   **Repository**: The .git directory containing version control data.

4. **Generating and Adding SSH Keys (Optional for Remote Repositories)**

   o   Generate an SSH key:

   bash

```
ssh-keygen -t rsa -b 4096 -C "your.email@example.com"
```

- o Add the key to your SSH agent:

bash

```
eval "$(ssh-agent -s)"
ssh-add ~/.ssh/id_rsa
```

- o Add the public key to Git hosting services (e.g., GitHub, GitLab).

13.2 Basic Git Operations for Programmers

1. **Initializing a Git Repository**
   - o Create a new Git repository:

   bash

   ```
   git init
   ```

   - o Clone an existing repository:

   bash

   ```
   git clone [repository_url]
   ```

2. **Adding and Committing Changes**

- Check the current status of the repository:

bash

git status

- Add files to the staging area:

bash

git add file.txt
git add . # Add all changes in the current directory

- Commit changes with a message:

bash

git commit -m "Initial commit"

3. **Viewing Repository History**

- View commit history:

bash

git log

- Show a concise history:

bash

git log --oneline

4. **Branching and Merging**

　　o　Create a new branch:

```bash
git branch new-feature
```

　　o　Switch to the new branch:

```bash
git checkout new-feature
```

　　o　Merge branches:

```bash
git checkout main
git merge new-feature
```

5. **Working with Remote Repositories**

　　o　Add a remote repository:

```bash
git remote add origin [repository_url]
```

　　o　Push changes to the remote repository:

```bash
```

git push -u origin main

   o   Pull changes from the remote repository:

bash

git pull origin main

6. Resolving Merge Conflicts

   o   Identify conflicts during a merge:

       ▪   Git will mark conflicting sections in affected files.

   o   Edit the files to resolve conflicts, then stage and commit:

bash

git add resolved_file.txt
git commit

13.3 Integrating Git into Your Development Workflow

1. Best Practices for Git

   o   Commit often with meaningful messages:

       ▪   Example: git commit -m "Add feature X to improve performance"

   o   Use branches for feature development:

- Keep main or master clean for production-ready code.
  - Pull frequently to stay updated with the latest changes.

2. **Collaborating with Teams**
   - Fork and clone repositories for independent development.
   - Use pull requests (PRs) to contribute changes to a shared repository.
   - Review and test code changes before merging.

3. **Automating Git Operations**
   - Use .gitignore to exclude unnecessary files from version control:
     - Example:

       bash

       ```
       node_modules/
       *.log
       ```

   - Automate deployment workflows with Git hooks:
     - Example: A pre-commit hook to check for code formatting.

4. **Git Tools and Extensions**
   - Use graphical Git clients like **GitKraken** or **Sourcetree** for visualization.

o Integrate Git with IDEs like Visual Studio Code for a seamless experience.

5. **Real-World Use Case**

o A developer creates a branch for a new feature, implements changes, and pushes the branch to a remote repository. A pull request is opened, reviewed by team members, and merged into the main branch.

13.4 Practical Examples and Exercises

1. **Examples**

o Create a repository, add a file, and push it to a remote repository.

o Resolve a merge conflict during a branch merge.

o Set up a .gitignore file for a Python project.

2. **Hands-On Exercises**

o Clone an open-source project from GitHub and explore its history.

o Create a branch, make changes, and merge it into the main branch.

o Use git log to identify the commit that introduced a bug.

3. **Common Troubleshooting**

- o Fix "detached HEAD" state:

  bash

  git checkout main

- o Handle errors during a push:
    - Check remote URL: git remote -v.
    - Use git pull to sync with the remote branch.

13.5

1. **Key Takeaways**
    - o Git is essential for version control, enabling collaborative development and project management.
    - o Mastering basic operations and workflows ensures efficient development.
    - o Integration with tools and best practices enhances productivity.

2. **Next Steps**
    - o Explore advanced Git features like rebasing, stashing, and submodules.
    - o Learn about CI/CD pipelines and their integration with Git.

Chapter 14: Development Tools on Linux

This chapter explores essential development tools on Linux, focusing on setting up programming environments, selecting editors and IDEs, and leveraging debugging and performance monitoring tools to optimize development workflows.

14.1 Setting Up Programming Environments (Python, C++, Java, etc.)

1. **General Steps for Setting Up Programming Environments**
   - Install compilers or interpreters.
   - Configure environment variables (e.g., PATH).
   - Test the setup with a "Hello, World!" program.

2. **Setting Up Python**
   - Install Python:
     - **Debian/Ubuntu**:

       bash

       ```
       sudo apt update
       sudo apt install python3 python3-pip
       ```

     - Verify installation:

bash

python3 --version

- o Set up a virtual environment:

bash

python3 -m venv myenv
source myenv/bin/activate

- o Install packages with pip:

bash

pip install numpy pandas

3. Setting Up C++

- o Install GCC (GNU Compiler Collection):

bash

sudo apt install g++

- o Compile and run a program:

bash

g++ -o hello hello.cpp
./hello

o Debugging with gdb:

bash

gdb ./hello

4. Setting Up Java

o Install the JDK:

bash

sudo apt install openjdk-11-jdk

o Verify installation:

bash

java -version

o Compile and run a program:

bash

javac HelloWorld.java
java HelloWorld

5. Setting Up Additional Languages

o **Node.js** (JavaScript):

bash

sudo apt install nodejs npm

o **Ruby**:

bash

sudo apt install ruby

o **Go**:

bash

sudo apt install golang

14.2 Editors and IDEs: Vim, VS Code, etc.

1. **Vim**

   o **Overview**:
      - A powerful, terminal-based text editor.
   o **Basic Commands**:
      - Enter insert mode: Press i.
      - Save and exit: Press Esc, then type :wq.
      - Quit without saving: :q!.
   o **Customization**:
      - Configure .vimrc for personalized settings.
      - Install plugins with tools like vim-plug.

2. **Visual Studio Code**

   o **Overview**:

- A popular, extensible editor with support for multiple languages.

- o **Installation**:
  - Download and install from the official website or use a package manager.
  - Example:

```bash
sudo apt install code
```

- o **Features**:
  - Extensions for Python, C++, Java, etc.
  - Integrated terminal and debugging tools.

3. **Other Editors and IDEs**

- o **Atom**:
  - A lightweight editor with Git integration.
  - Install:

```bash
sudo snap install atom
```

- o **JetBrains IDEs**:
  - IntelliJ IDEA for Java, PyCharm for Python, etc.
  - Download from JetBrains.

- o **Eclipse**:

- A popular IDE for Java and other languages.
- Install:

bash

sudo apt install eclipse

4. **Choosing the Right Editor/IDE**

   o Vim or Nano: Lightweight and fast for quick edits.

   o VS Code: Ideal for general-purpose development with modern features.

   o IntelliJ IDEA or Eclipse: Best for Java and enterprise-level projects.

14.3 Debugging and Performance Monitoring Tools

1. **Debugging Tools**

   o **GDB (GNU Debugger)**:

      - Debug C/C++ programs.
      - Example:

   bash

   gdb ./program
   run

   o **Python Debugger (pdb)**:

- Debug Python scripts:

bash

python3 -m pdb script.py

o **Valgrind**:
  - Detect memory leaks in C/C++ programs.

bash

valgrind ./program

o **Integrated Debuggers in IDEs**:
  - Use built-in debugging features in VS Code or IntelliJ.

2. **Performance Monitoring Tools**
   o **Top and Htop**:
     - Monitor system resources in real-time.
     - Install htop:

bash

sudo apt install htop

o **Perf**:
  - Analyze CPU and memory usage:

bash

perf stat ./program

- o **System Monitoring Tools**:
  - ▪ iotop: Monitor disk I/O usage.
  - ▪ nmon: Comprehensive system performance monitoring.

3. **Code Profilers**
   - o **Python Profiling**:
     - ▪ Use cProfile:

bash

python3 -m cProfile script.py

   - o **Java Profiling**:
     - ▪ Use VisualVM or JProfiler.
   - o **C++ Profiling**:
     - ▪ Use tools like gprof:

bash

g++ -pg program.cpp -o program
./program
gprof program gmon.out > analysis.txt

14.4 Practical Examples and Exercises

1. **Examples**

   o Set up and run a Python virtual environment.

   o Create and debug a C++ program using gdb.

   o Monitor system performance during a CPU-intensive task with htop.

2. **Hands-On Exercises**

   o Write and run a "Hello, World!" program in Python, C++, and Java.

   o Customize VS Code with extensions for your preferred programming language.

   o Use perf to analyze the performance of a sample program.

3. **Common Troubleshooting**

   o Fix "Command not found" errors by checking installation paths.

   o Resolve dependency issues by installing missing libraries.

   o Address high resource usage by identifying and optimizing problematic processes.

14.5

1. **Key Takeaways**

- o Setting up programming environments on Linux enables efficient development across multiple languages.
- o Editors like Vim and IDEs like VS Code cater to diverse developer needs.
- o Debugging and performance monitoring tools are essential for optimizing and troubleshooting code.

2. **Next Steps**

- o Explore more advanced IDE features like version control integration.
- o Learn additional debugging techniques for specific programming languages.
- o Experiment with advanced profiling tools to optimize resource usage.

This chapter provides a solid foundation for using Linux as a development platform, equipping readers with tools and techniques for a productive workflow.

Chapter 15: Understanding Linux Services and Daemons

This chapter introduces Linux services and daemons, delves into systemd and other init systems, and demonstrates how to manage services effectively using systemctl with practical examples.

15.1 Introduction to systemd and Init Systems

1. **What Are Services and Daemons?**

   o **Services**:

      ▪ Programs that run in the background to provide specific functionalities (e.g., web server, database server).

   o **Daemons**:

      ▪ Background processes often started at boot time and managed by the init system.

      ▪ Common naming convention: Ends with d (e.g., httpd, sshd).

2. **Overview of Init Systems**

   o **Init Systems**:

      ▪ Responsible for initializing services during system startup and managing them while the system is running.

- o **Legacy Init (SysVinit)**:
  - Early init system using shell scripts in /etc/rc.d directories.
- o **Upstart**:
  - An event-based replacement for SysVinit, used in older Ubuntu versions.
- o **systemd**:
  - Modern init system adopted by most Linux distributions.
  - Offers faster boot times, parallel service startup, and advanced service management.

3. **Features of systemd**
   - o Unit-based architecture:
     - Units represent services, targets, sockets, and devices.
   - o Centralized service management with systemctl.
   - o Logging and monitoring with journald.

15.2 Managing Services with systemctl

1. **Viewing Services**
   - o List all active services:

   bash

```
systemctl list-units --type=service
```

- o Check the status of a specific service:

bash

```
systemctl status apache2
```

2. Starting and Stopping Services

- o Start a service:

bash

```
sudo systemctl start apache2
```

- o Stop a service:

bash

```
sudo systemctl stop apache2
```

3. Enabling and Disabling Services

- o Enable a service to start at boot:

bash

```
sudo systemctl enable apache2
```

- o Disable a service:

bash

```
sudo systemctl disable apache2
```

4. Restarting and Reloading Services

o Restart a service:

```
bash
```

```
sudo systemctl restart apache2
```

o Reload a service's configuration without stopping it:

```
bash
```

```
sudo systemctl reload apache2
```

5. Analyzing Failed Services

o List failed services:

```
bash
```

```
systemctl --failed
```

o View detailed logs for a service:

```
bash
```

```
journalctl -u apache2
```

15.3 Practical Examples of Service Management

1. **Managing a Web Server**
   - Start the Apache web server:

     bash

     sudo systemctl start apache2

   - Check its status:

     bash

     systemctl status apache2

   - Enable it to start on boot:

     bash

     sudo systemctl enable apache2

2. **Configuring a Database Service**
   - Restart the MySQL service after updating its configuration:

     bash

     sudo systemctl restart mysql

   - View detailed logs for troubleshooting:

     bash

journalctl -u mysql

3. Automating Log Rotation

o   Enable and start the logrotate service:

bash

```
sudo systemctl enable logrotate
sudo systemctl start logrotate
```

4. Disabling Unnecessary Services

o   List enabled services:

bash

```
systemctl list-unit-files --type=service | grep enabled
```

o   Disable a service you don't need:

bash

```
sudo systemctl disable cups
```

5. Monitoring System Performance

o   Start the cron service to schedule periodic tasks:

bash

```
sudo systemctl start cron
```

o   Ensure the service is active and running:

bash

systemctl is-active cron

15.4 Common Troubleshooting Scenarios

1. **Service Fails to Start**

   o   Check for errors in the service status:

   bash

   systemctl status [service_name]

   o   View logs for more information:

   bash

   journalctl -xe

2. **Service Doesn't Start at Boot**

   o   Ensure the service is enabled:

   bash

   sudo systemctl enable [service_name]

3. **Service Is Running but Not Responding**

   o   Restart the service:

bash

sudo systemctl restart [service_name]

   o   Check the service's configuration file for issues.

15.5 Practical Examples and Exercises

1. **Examples**
   - Configure and manage the Nginx web server:
     - Install:

       bash

       sudo apt install nginx

     - Start and enable:

       bash

       sudo systemctl start nginx
       sudo systemctl enable nginx

   - Monitor and troubleshoot failed services.

2. **Hands-On Exercises**

- o Create a script that lists all active services and their statuses.
- o Identify and disable unnecessary services on your system.
- o Set up and configure a service to run automatically at startup.

3. **Common Troubleshooting**

- o Fix "Permission Denied" errors by using sudo when managing services.
- o Diagnose slow startup times with systemd-analyze blame.

15.6

1. **Key Takeaways**

- o systemd is the standard init system for managing Linux services and daemons.
- o systemctl provides powerful and user-friendly commands for service management.
- o Understanding service logs and troubleshooting ensures a stable and reliable system.

2. **Next Steps**

- o Explore advanced systemd features, such as timers and custom unit files.

o   Learn how to create and manage custom services for specific applications.

This chapter equips readers with the skills to manage Linux services and daemons effectively, ensuring smooth operation of critical applications.

Chapter 16: Working with Logs

This chapter focuses on the importance of log files in Linux, explains how to access and analyze logs using tools like journalctl and log files, and demonstrates techniques for automating log management.

16.1 Importance of Log Files in Linux

1. **What Are Log Files?**

    o Log files are records of system, application, and user activities.

    o They provide insights into system health, performance, and security.

2. **Types of Log Files**

    o **System Logs**: Kernel messages, boot logs, etc. (e.g., /var/log/syslog).

    o **Application Logs**: Logs for specific services or programs (e.g., /var/log/apache2/access.log).

    o **Security Logs**: Records of authentication and authorization activities (e.g., /var/log/auth.log).

    o **Custom Logs**: User-defined logs for specific scripts or applications.

3. **Why Are Logs Important?**

- o **Troubleshooting**: Diagnose issues by analyzing error messages.

- o **Monitoring**: Track system performance and user activity.

- o **Security**: Detect unauthorized access and potential threats.

- o **Compliance**: Maintain records for audits and legal requirements.

16.2 Accessing and Analyzing Logs with journalctl and Log Files

1. **Systemd Journals with journalctl**

   - o **Accessing Logs**:
     - View all logs:

       bash

       journalctl

     - View recent logs:

       bash

       journalctl -r

   - o **Filtering Logs**:
     - By date:

bash

journalctl --since "2023-01-01" --until "2023-01-31"

- **By service:**

bash

journalctl -u apache2

- **By priority:**

bash

journalctl -p err

o **Monitoring Logs in Real Time**:

bash

journalctl -f

2. **Analyzing Logs in /var/log**

   o **Common Log Files**:
   - /var/log/syslog: General system activity logs.
   - /var/log/auth.log: Authentication logs.
   - /var/log/dmesg: Kernel ring buffer logs.

   o **Viewing Logs**:
   - Use cat, less, or tail:

bash

tail -f /var/log/syslog

- o **Searching Log Content**:
    - Use grep to find specific entries:

bash

grep "ERROR" /var/log/syslog

    - Combine with awk or sed for detailed analysis:

bash

grep "ERROR" /var/log/syslog | awk '{print $1, $2, $3}'

3. **Log Rotation**

- o Managed by the logrotate utility:
    - Configuration files in /etc/logrotate.d/.
- o Example of a logrotate configuration:

plaintext

```
/var/log/myapp.log {
  daily
  rotate 7
  compress
  missingok
```

notifempty

}

16.3 Automating Log Management

1. Automating Log Rotation

- Install and configure logrotate:

  bash

  sudo apt install logrotate

- Run logrotate manually for testing:

  bash

  sudo logrotate -v /etc/logrotate.conf

2. Archiving and Compressing Logs

- Use gzip to compress old logs:

  bash

  gzip /var/log/myapp.log

- Automate compression with a script:

  bash

  #!/bin/bash

```
find /var/log/myapp/ -name "*.log" -mtime +7 -exec gzip {} \;
```

3. Deleting Old Logs

o Delete logs older than a specific number of days:

bash

```
find /var/log/myapp/ -name "*.log" -mtime +30 -delete
```

4. Monitoring Log Activity

o Set up a cron job to analyze logs periodically:

bash

```
0 2 * * * /usr/bin/grep "ERROR" /var/log/syslog >> /var/log/errors.log
```

5. Using Centralized Log Management

o Tools like **ELK Stack (Elasticsearch, Logstash, Kibana)**:

   ▪ Aggregate, visualize, and analyze logs.

o **Syslog-ng** or **rsyslog**:

   ▪ Send logs to a central server for unified management.

16.4 Practical Examples and Exercises

1. **Examples**

   o Use journalctl to filter and view logs for a specific service (e.g., SSH).

   o Rotate logs for a custom application using logrotate.

   o Create a script to archive logs older than 30 days.

2. **Hands-On Exercises**

   o Analyze logs to identify failed login attempts.

   o Configure logrotate for an application and test its behavior.

   o Set up a cron job to generate a daily of critical system logs.

3. **Common Troubleshooting**

   o Fix "Permission Denied" errors when accessing logs by using sudo.

   o Resolve missing logs by verifying service logging configurations.

   o Handle large log files by compressing or splitting them into smaller parts.

16.5

1. **Key Takeaways**

   o Logs are essential for troubleshooting, monitoring, and securing Linux systems.

- o Tools like journalctl and manual log analysis provide comprehensive insights.
- o Automating log management ensures efficient storage and retrieval of log data.

2. **Next Steps**

- o Explore centralized log management solutions for large-scale systems.
- o Learn to customize log formats and configurations for specific applications.
- o Practice writing scripts to automate log analysis and reporting.

This chapter equips readers with essential skills to work with logs effectively, ensuring they can monitor, troubleshoot, and manage Linux systems with confidence.

Chapter 17: Linux Networking for Web Development

This chapter covers the foundational knowledge for web development on Linux, including setting up local web servers, configuring databases, and hosting a basic website. These skills are essential for developers building and deploying web applications.

17.1 Setting Up Local Web Servers (Apache, Nginx)

1. **Understanding Web Servers**
   - Web servers handle HTTP requests and serve web pages to users.
   - Popular Linux web servers:
     - **Apache**: Reliable and feature-rich.
     - **Nginx**: Lightweight and efficient, excellent for handling high traffic.

2. **Installing Apache**
   - Install Apache:

   bash

   ```
   sudo apt update
   sudo apt install apache2
   ```

o   Start and enable the service:

bash

```
sudo systemctl start apache2
sudo systemctl enable apache2
```

o   Test the setup:

- Open a browser and visit http://localhost to see the default Apache page.

o   Configure Apache:

- Modify configuration files in /etc/apache2/.
- Example: Set up a virtual host:

plaintext

```
<VirtualHost *:80>
   ServerName example.com
   DocumentRoot /var/www/html/example
</VirtualHost>
```

- Enable the configuration:

bash

```
sudo a2ensite example.conf
sudo systemctl reload apache2
```

3. **Installing Nginx**

o   Install Nginx:

bash

sudo apt install nginx

o Start and enable the service:

bash

sudo systemctl start nginx
sudo systemctl enable nginx

o Test the setup:

- Open a browser and visit http://localhost to see the default Nginx page.

o Configure Nginx:

- Modify configuration files in /etc/nginx/sites-available/.

- Example: Set up a server block:

plaintext

```
server {
  listen 80;
  server_name example.com;
  root /var/www/html/example;
  index index.html;
}
```

- Enable the configuration:

bash

sudo   ln   -s   /etc/nginx/sites-available/example
/etc/nginx/sites-enabled/
sudo systemctl reload nginx

17.2 Configuring Databases (MySQL, PostgreSQL)

1. **Installing MySQL**

   o   Install MySQL:

   bash

   sudo apt install mysql-server

   o   Secure the installation:

   bash

   sudo mysql_secure_installation

   o   Log in to MySQL:

   bash

   sudo mysql

   o   Create a database and user:

   sql

CREATE DATABASE myapp;

CREATE USER 'myuser'@'localhost' IDENTIFIED BY 'mypassword';

GRANT ALL PRIVILEGES ON myapp.* TO 'myuser'@'localhost';

FLUSH PRIVILEGES;

2. Installing PostgreSQL

o Install PostgreSQL:

bash

```
sudo apt install postgresql postgresql-contrib
```

o Log in to PostgreSQL:

bash

```
sudo -i -u postgres
psql
```

o Create a database and user:

sql

```
CREATE DATABASE myapp;
CREATE USER myuser WITH PASSWORD 'mypassword';
GRANT ALL PRIVILEGES ON DATABASE myapp TO myuser;
```

3. Connecting Web Servers to Databases

- Install necessary PHP modules for database connectivity:
  - MySQL: sudo apt install php-mysql.
  - PostgreSQL: sudo apt install php-pgsql.
- Test database connectivity with a PHP script:

php

```php
<?php
$conn = new mysqli("localhost", "myuser", "mypassword", "myapp");
if ($conn->connect_error) {
  die("Connection failed: " . $conn->connect_error);
}
echo "Connected successfully";
?>
```

17.3 Hosting a Basic Website on Linux

1. Preparing the Website Files

- Place website files in the document root:
  - Apache: /var/www/html/.
  - Nginx: /var/www/html/.
- Example:

bash

```
sudo mkdir -p /var/www/html/example
sudo cp -r ~/mywebsite/* /var/www/html/example/
```

2. Configuring the Web Server

- **Apache**:
  - Create a virtual host configuration in /etc/apache2/sites-available/example.conf.
  - Enable the configuration:

    bash

    ```
    sudo a2ensite example.conf
    sudo systemctl reload apache2
    ```

- **Nginx**:
  - Create a server block configuration in /etc/nginx/sites-available/example.
  - Enable the configuration:

    bash

    ```
    sudo ln -s /etc/nginx/sites-available/example
    /etc/nginx/sites-enabled/
    sudo systemctl reload nginx
    ```

3. Testing the Website

- Open a browser and visit http://localhost or the server's IP address.
- Troubleshoot issues by checking logs:

- • Apache: /var/log/apache2/error.log.
- • Nginx: /var/log/nginx/error.log.

4. Securing the Website with HTTPS

- o Install Certbot for Let's Encrypt:

bash

```
sudo apt install certbot python3-certbot-apache  # For Apache
sudo apt install certbot python3-certbot-nginx   # For Nginx
```

- o Obtain and configure an SSL certificate:

bash

```
sudo certbot --apache   # For Apache
sudo certbot --nginx    # For Nginx
```

17.4 Practical Examples and Exercises

1. Examples

- o Set up a simple HTML website with Apache.
- o Configure an Nginx server to serve static files.
- o Connect a PHP application to a MySQL database.

2. Hands-On Exercises

- o Create a virtual host or server block for a custom domain.

- o Set up a basic WordPress website on Apache or Nginx.
- o Configure SSL for your website using Let's Encrypt.

3. Common Troubleshooting

- o Fix "403 Forbidden" errors by checking file permissions.
- o Diagnose "502 Bad Gateway" errors by verifying backend services.
- o Resolve database connection issues by checking user credentials and permissions.

17.5

1. Key Takeaways

- o Linux is a robust platform for setting up web servers and hosting websites.
- o Tools like Apache, Nginx, MySQL, and PostgreSQL are essential for web development.
- o Proper configuration and security practices ensure reliable and safe hosting.

2. Next Steps

- o Explore advanced web server configurations like reverse proxies and load balancing.

- o Learn to deploy websites using containerization tools like Docker.
- o Integrate continuous deployment pipelines for automated updates.

This chapter equips readers with the knowledge to set up and configure a complete web development environment on Linux, from web servers to databases and hosting.

Chapter 18: Introduction to Containers and Virtualization

This chapter introduces the concepts of containers and virtualization, with a focus on Docker and VirtualBox. It covers their setup and practical applications in development workflows, providing real-world examples of how these technologies streamline modern development processes.

18.1 Basics of Docker and Containerization

1. **What Are Containers?**
   - Lightweight, portable environments that package applications and dependencies.
   - Key benefits:
     - **Isolation**: Each container operates independently.
     - **Portability**: Run containers on any system with Docker installed.
     - **Efficiency**: Containers share the host OS kernel, reducing overhead compared to virtual machines.

2. **Introduction to Docker**
   - Docker is the most popular containerization platform.

- Components of Docker:
  - **Docker Engine**: Core technology to build and run containers.
  - **Docker Images**: Blueprints for creating containers.
  - **Docker Containers**: Running instances of images.
  - **Docker Hub**: Repository for sharing images.

3. **Installing Docker on Linux**
   - Install Docker:

   bash

   ```
   sudo apt update
   sudo apt install docker.io
   ```

   - Start Docker and enable it at boot:

   bash

   ```
   sudo systemctl start docker
   sudo systemctl enable docker
   ```

   - Verify the installation:

   bash

   ```
   docker --version
   ```

4. Basic Docker Commands

○ Pull an image:

bash

docker pull ubuntu

○ Run a container:

bash

docker run -it ubuntu

○ List running containers:

bash

docker ps

○ Stop and remove a container:

bash

docker stop container_id
docker rm container_id

18.2 Setting Up and Using Virtual Machines with VirtualBox

1. What Are Virtual Machines?

- o Virtual machines (VMs) simulate entire operating systems, allowing multiple OSes to run on a single host.
- o Use cases:
  - Testing software on different OSes.
  - Creating isolated development environments.
  - Running legacy applications.

2. **Installing VirtualBox**

   - o Install VirtualBox:

   bash

   ```
   sudo apt update
   sudo apt install virtualbox
   ```

   - o Verify the installation:

   bash

   ```
   virtualbox --help
   ```

3. **Creating a Virtual Machine**

   - o Launch VirtualBox and click **New**.
   - o Configure the VM:
     - Name: Choose a descriptive name (e.g., "Ubuntu Dev VM").
     - Type: Select the OS type (e.g., Linux).

- Memory: Allocate RAM (e.g., 4GB for Ubuntu).
- Storage: Attach a virtual hard disk.
  o Install the guest OS:
    - Attach an ISO file to the VM and start it.
    - Follow the OS installation steps.

4. Using Virtual Machines

o Start, pause, and stop VMs from the VirtualBox interface or CLI:

bash

```
VBoxManage startvm "Ubuntu Dev VM"
VBoxManage controlvm "Ubuntu Dev VM" poweroff
```

o Configure shared folders:
  - Install Guest Additions for better integration.
  - Mount shared folders for file sharing between the host and VM.

5. Comparison: Containers vs. Virtual Machines

o Containers are faster and use fewer resources, ideal for microservices and CI/CD pipelines.
o Virtual machines provide complete OS isolation, better for legacy applications or OS-level testing.

18.3 Real-World Examples of Using Containers in Development

1. **Developing a Web Application**
   o Use Docker to set up a development stack:
     ▪ Pull images for Nginx, Node.js, and MySQL:

     bash

     ```
     docker pull nginx
     docker pull node
     docker pull mysql
     ```

     ▪ Create and link containers:

     bash

     ```
     docker network create dev-network
     docker run --name webserver --network dev-network
     -d nginx
     docker run --name database --network dev-network -e
     MYSQL_ROOT_PASSWORD=root -d mysql
     ```

2. **Testing Software in Isolated Environments**
   o Create a container to test an application with specific dependencies:

   bash

   ```
   docker run -it python:3.10 bash
   ```

3. **Using Docker Compose for Multi-Container Applications**

   o Write a docker-compose.yml file to define a multi-container setup:

   yaml

   ```yaml
   version: '3'
   services:
    web:
      image: nginx
      ports:
       - "8080:80"
    db:
      image: mysql
      environment:
        MYSQL_ROOT_PASSWORD: root
   ```

   o Start all services:

   bash

   ```bash
   docker-compose up
   ```

4. **Continuous Integration and Deployment (CI/CD)**

   o Integrate Docker with CI/CD pipelines to test and deploy applications:

      ▪ Build an image:

bash

docker build -t myapp .

- Push the image to a registry:

bash

docker push myregistry/myapp

18.4 Practical Examples and Exercises

1. **Examples**
   - Set up a WordPress website with Docker Compose.
   - Create a VM with Ubuntu using VirtualBox and install a development stack (e.g., LAMP).
   - Run a Node.js application in a Docker container.

2. **Hands-On Exercises**
   - Write a Dockerfile to containerize a simple Python application.
   - Create and configure a VirtualBox VM for testing a multi-OS application.
   - Use Docker Compose to deploy a multi-container application with Nginx and MySQL.

3. **Common Troubleshooting**
   - Fix permission issues with Docker by adding your user to the Docker group:

bash

sudo usermod -aG docker $USER

- o Resolve network connectivity issues in VirtualBox by configuring NAT or Bridged networking.
- o Diagnose container errors by inspecting logs:

bash

docker logs container_id

18.5

1. **Key Takeaways**
   - o Containers and virtualization provide flexible, efficient environments for development and testing.
   - o Docker simplifies application deployment and scalability with lightweight containers.
   - o VirtualBox is a powerful tool for creating and managing fully isolated operating systems.

2. **Next Steps**
   - o Explore advanced Docker features like volumes, networks, and custom Dockerfiles.
   - o Learn about orchestration tools like Kubernetes for managing containerized applications.

o   Use VirtualBox snapshots to create and manage development checkpoints.

This chapter provides a comprehensive introduction to containers and virtualization, equipping readers with practical skills to enhance their development workflows.

Chapter 19: Linux Security Essentials

This chapter introduces the fundamental security practices for Linux systems, including configuring firewalls, adopting security best practices for developers, and encrypting data and securing SSH access.

19.1 Configuring Firewalls with UFW and iptables

1. **Understanding Firewalls**

   o Firewalls control incoming and outgoing network traffic based on predefined rules.

   o **UFW (Uncomplicated Firewall)**: A user-friendly front-end for iptables.

   o **iptables**: A powerful tool for managing Linux kernel packet filtering.

2. **Setting Up UFW**

   o Install UFW (if not already installed):

   bash

   ```
   sudo apt update
   sudo apt install ufw
   ```

   o Enable UFW:

bash

sudo ufw enable

- o Allow or deny traffic:
    - Allow HTTP:

        bash

        sudo ufw allow 80/tcp

    - Deny all traffic by default:

        bash

        sudo ufw default deny

- o Check the firewall status:

    bash

    sudo ufw status

- o Example UFW configuration for a web server:

    bash

    sudo ufw allow ssh
    sudo ufw allow http
    sudo ufw allow https
    sudo ufw enable

3. Using iptables

- View existing rules:

  bash

  sudo iptables -L -v

- Allow SSH traffic:

  bash

  sudo iptables -A INPUT -p tcp --dport 22 -j ACCEPT

- Block an IP address:

  bash

  sudo iptables -A INPUT -s 192.168.1.100 -j DROP

- Save iptables rules:

  bash

  sudo iptables-save > /etc/iptables/rules.v4

19.2 Security Best Practices for Developers

1. Keep the System Updated

- Regularly update packages to patch vulnerabilities:

bash

sudo apt update && sudo apt upgrade

2. **Use Secure Coding Practices**
   - o Validate all user inputs to prevent SQL injection and XSS attacks.
   - o Avoid hardcoding sensitive data (e.g., API keys) in your code.

3. **Implement Principle of Least Privilege**
   - o Assign minimal permissions required for each user or process.
   - o Example: Configure database users with access only to necessary tables.

4. **Use Secure Passwords**
   - o Enforce strong password policies:
     - ▪ At least 12 characters, with a mix of upper and lowercase letters, numbers, and symbols.
   - o Use tools like pwgen to generate secure passwords:

bash

sudo apt install pwgen
pwgen -s 16 1

5. **Monitor Logs for Suspicious Activity**
   - o Regularly review authentication logs:

161

bash

sudo cat /var/log/auth.log | grep "Failed password"

6. Disable Unnecessary Services

- o List all active services:

bash

systemctl list-units --type=service

- o Disable unused services:

bash

sudo systemctl disable [service_name]

19.3 Encrypting Data and Securing SSH

1. Encrypting Data

- o **Using GPG for File Encryption**:
  - Encrypt a file:

bash

gpg -c file.txt

  - Decrypt a file:

bash

gpg file.txt.gpg

- o **Encrypting Disk Partitions with LUKS**:
  - Install cryptsetup:

    bash

    sudo apt install cryptsetup

  - Set up LUKS encryption on a partition:

    bash

    sudo cryptsetup luksFormat /dev/sdX

  - Open the encrypted partition:

    bash

    sudo cryptsetup luksOpen /dev/sdX encrypted_partition

2. Securing SSH Access

- o **Disable Root Login**:
  - Edit /etc/ssh/sshd_config and set:

    plaintext

PermitRootLogin no

- Restart the SSH service:

bash

sudo systemctl restart ssh

o **Change the Default SSH Port**:

  - Edit /etc/ssh/sshd_config and set:

plaintext

Port 2222

  - Restart the SSH service:

bash

sudo systemctl restart ssh

o **Set Up SSH Key Authentication**:

  - Generate an SSH key pair:

bash

ssh-keygen   -t   rsa   -b   4096   -C
"your.email@example.com"

  - Copy the public key to the server:

bash

ssh-copy-id user@remote_server

- Disable password authentication:

plaintext

PasswordAuthentication no

3. **Using Fail2Ban to Prevent Brute Force Attacks**
   o Install Fail2Ban:

bash

sudo apt install fail2ban

   o Enable and start the service:

bash

sudo systemctl enable fail2ban
sudo systemctl start fail2ban

   o Configure Fail2Ban rules in /etc/fail2ban/jail.local:

plaintext

[sshd]
enabled = true
maxretry = 5

bantime = 3600

19.4 Practical Examples and Exercises

1. **Examples**
   - o Set up UFW to allow SSH, HTTP, and HTTPS traffic while blocking all other traffic.
   - o Encrypt a sensitive file using GPG and decrypt it on another machine.
   - o Configure SSH to use a non-default port and disable root login.

2. **Hands-On Exercises**
   - o Use iptables to block a specific IP address and allow all other traffic.
   - o Install and configure Fail2Ban to monitor SSH login attempts.
   - o Set up LUKS encryption for a USB drive and test its functionality.

3. **Common Troubleshooting**
   - o Fix SSH connection issues by verifying firewall rules.
   - o Resolve "Permission Denied" errors when accessing encrypted files by checking user ownership.
   - o Test firewall configurations using tools like nmap.

19.5

1. **Key Takeaways**

   o Linux security relies on a layered approach, combining firewalls, encryption, and secure configurations.

   o UFW simplifies firewall management, while iptables offers advanced control.

   o SSH is a critical entry point that must be secured with keys, non-default ports, and tools like Fail2Ban.

2. **Next Steps**

   o Explore advanced firewall rules with iptables and nftables.

   o Implement intrusion detection systems (e.g., Snort or Suricata).

   o Learn about SELinux or AppArmor for fine-grained security controls.

This chapter equips readers with essential tools and practices to secure Linux systems and protect data effectively.

Chapter 20: Troubleshooting Linux Systems

This chapter addresses common Linux system issues and provides tools and techniques for diagnosing and resolving them. It also covers backup and recovery strategies to mitigate data loss during troubleshooting.

20.1 Common Issues and How to Resolve Them

1. **System Won't Boot**
   - **Symptoms**:
     - Blank screen, GRUB errors, or kernel panics.
   - **Resolution**:
     - Check GRUB configuration:

       bash

       sudo nano /etc/default/grub

     - Update GRUB:

       bash

       sudo update-grub

- Boot into recovery mode from the GRUB menu.
- Inspect logs for errors:

bash

journalctl -b

2. **Network Connectivity Issues**

   o **Symptoms**:
      - No internet access or inability to reach a specific host.
   o **Resolution**:
      - Check network interface status:

      bash

      ip addr

      - Restart the network service:

      bash

      sudo systemctl restart networking

      - Test DNS resolution:

      bash

ping google.com

- Verify routes:

bash

ip route

3. **High CPU or Memory Usage**
   - **Symptoms**:
     - System slowdowns or unresponsive applications.
   - **Resolution**:
     - Identify resource-hogging processes:

bash

top
htop

     - Kill the offending process:

bash

sudo kill [PID]

4. **Disk Space Issues**
   - **Symptoms**:
     - "No space left on device" errors.

- o **Resolution**:
  - Check disk usage:

    bash

    df -h

  - Find large files:

    bash

    sudo du -sh /path/*

  - Clear unused logs:

    bash

    sudo journalctl --vacuum-size=100M

5. **Package Installation Failures**
   - o **Symptoms**:
     - Dependency errors or broken packages.
   - o **Resolution**:
     - Fix broken packages:

       bash

       sudo apt --fix-broken install

     - Clean package cache:

bash

sudo apt clean

- Update package lists:

bash

sudo apt update

20.2 Using Diagnostic Commands (dmesg, strace)

1. **dmesg: Kernel Ring Buffer Logs**
   o **Purpose**:
     - View messages from the Linux kernel, such as hardware issues or driver errors.
   o **Usage**:
     - Display all messages:

bash

dmesg

     - Filter messages for specific keywords:

bash

dmesg | grep "error"

- Monitor new messages in real-time:

bash

dmesg -w

2. strace: **System Call Tracer**

- **Purpose**:
  - Debug application issues by tracing system calls and signals.
- **Usage**:
  - Trace a command:

bash

strace ls

  - Log output to a file:

bash

strace -o trace.log my_program

  - Identify missing files or permissions:

bash

strace -e open ls

3. **Other Useful Diagnostic Tools**

- o **lsof**: List open files by a process:

  bash

  lsof -p [PID]

- o **iotop**: Monitor disk I/O activity:

  bash

  sudo iotop

- o **systemctl**: Check service status:

  bash

  systemctl status [service_name]

20.3 Backup and Recovery Techniques

1. **Backup Strategies**
   - o **Full Backups**:
     - Backs up all files.
     - Example: Using tar:

       bash

       tar -czf backup.tar.gz /path/to/directory

- **Incremental Backups**:
  - Backs up only files changed since the last backup.
  - Tools like rsync:

    bash

    rsync -av --progress /source /destination

- **Automating Backups**:
  - Schedule backups with cron:

    bash

    0 2 * * * tar -czf /backup/$(date +\%Y\%m\%d).tar.gz /data

2. Recovery Techniques

- Restore from a tar backup:

  bash

  tar -xzf backup.tar.gz -C /restore/path

- Restore individual files with rsync:

  bash

  rsync -av /backup /original

3. Creating System Snapshots

  o Use timeshift for system snapshots:

  ▪ Install timeshift:

bash

sudo apt install timeshift

  ▪ Create a snapshot:

bash

sudo timeshift --create

4. Recovering Deleted Files

  o Check the trash folder:

bash

~/.local/share/Trash

  o Use tools like testdisk:

bash

sudo apt install testdisk
sudo testdisk

20.4 Practical Examples and Exercises

1. **Examples**

   o Diagnose a system that fails to boot using dmesg.

   o Trace a faulty application with strace.

   o Automate daily backups of /home using cron.

2. **Hands-On Exercises**

   o Identify and terminate a process consuming high CPU using top.

   o Simulate a disk space issue and resolve it by clearing unnecessary files.

   o Use rsync to back up and restore a directory.

3. **Common Troubleshooting**

   o Resolve "Permission Denied" errors by verifying user privileges.

   o Address system hangs by inspecting kernel messages with dmesg.

   o Recover a corrupt GRUB configuration using a live CD.

20.5

1. **Key Takeaways**

   o Understanding common Linux issues and using diagnostic tools like dmesg and strace is essential for effective troubleshooting.

- o Implementing regular backups ensures data safety during system failures.
- o Familiarity with recovery techniques can significantly reduce downtime.

2. **Next Steps**

- o Explore advanced troubleshooting tools like perf for performance profiling.
- o Learn to configure automated backups using tools like rsnapshot or cloud services.
- o Practice resolving complex issues in a safe virtualized environment.

This chapter equips readers with essential troubleshooting skills, ensuring they can confidently handle Linux system issues and safeguard their data.

Chapter 21: Linux for DevOps

This chapter explores how Linux serves as the backbone for DevOps practices. It introduces essential DevOps tools, explains the creation of CI/CD pipelines with Jenkins and GitLab, and delves into infrastructure automation using Ansible.

21.1 Introduction to DevOps Tools on Linux

1. **Why Linux for DevOps?**

   o Linux's stability, flexibility, and open-source nature make it the preferred platform for DevOps tools.

   o Most DevOps tools, like Docker, Kubernetes, Jenkins, and Ansible, are native to Linux or integrate seamlessly with it.

2. **Popular DevOps Tools**

   o **Jenkins**: Automates CI/CD pipelines.

   o **GitLab CI/CD**: Integrated DevOps platform for version control and pipelines.

   o **Ansible**: Manages configuration, deployment, and automation.

   o **Terraform**: Provisions infrastructure as code.

   o **Prometheus and Grafana**: Monitor system and application performance.

3. **Setting Up a DevOps Environment**

o   Install necessary tools and dependencies:

bash

sudo apt update
sudo apt install docker git ansible

o   Configure SSH for secure communication:

bash

ssh-keygen -t rsa -b 4096 -C "your.email@example.com"

21.2 CI/CD Pipelines with Jenkins and GitLab

1. **Understanding CI/CD Pipelines**
   o   **Continuous Integration (CI)**:
      ▪   Automatically build and test code whenever changes are pushed.
   o   **Continuous Delivery (CD)**:
      ▪   Ensures code is always in a deployable state.
   o   **Continuous Deployment**:
      ▪   Automates the release of code to production.

2. **Setting Up Jenkins**
   o   **Install Jenkins**:

bash

```
sudo apt update
sudo apt install openjdk-11-jdk
curl -fsSL https://pkg.jenkins.io/debian-stable/jenkins.io.key |
sudo tee \
 /usr/share/keyrings/jenkins-keyring.asc > /dev/null
echo deb [signed-by=/usr/share/keyrings/jenkins-keyring.asc] \
 https://pkg.jenkins.io/debian-stable binary/ | sudo tee \
 /etc/apt/sources.list.d/jenkins.list > /dev/null
sudo apt update
sudo apt install jenkins
```

- o **Start and Access Jenkins**:

bash

```
sudo systemctl start jenkins
sudo systemctl enable jenkins
```

- - Access Jenkins at http://localhost:8080.
- o **Create a Pipeline**:
  - Install plugins for Git and Docker.
  - Use a sample Jenkinsfile:

groovy

```
pipeline {
  agent any
  stages {
    stage('Build') {
      steps {
```

```
        sh 'echo "Building..."'
      }
    }
    stage('Test') {
      steps {
        sh 'echo "Testing..."'
      }
    }
    stage('Deploy') {
      steps {
        sh 'echo "Deploying..."'
      }
    }
  }
}
```

3. **CI/CD with GitLab**

   o **Install GitLab**:

     - Follow installation instructions for your Linux distribution at GitLab Downloads.

   o **Create a GitLab CI/CD Pipeline**:

     - Add a .gitlab-ci.yml file to your repository:

     yaml

     ```
     stages:
       - build
       - test
       - deploy
     ```

```
build-job:
  stage: build
  script:
    - echo "Building the application"

test-job:
  stage: test
  script:
    - echo "Running tests"

deploy-job:
  stage: deploy
  script:
    - echo "Deploying application"
```

- o **Run Pipelines**:
  - Push changes to your GitLab repository to trigger the pipeline.
- o **Integrate with Docker**:
  - Use a docker executor in .gitlab-ci.yml to build and deploy containers.

21.3 Infrastructure as Code with Ansible

1. **What Is Infrastructure as Code (IaC)?**

o IaC allows managing and provisioning infrastructure using code, ensuring consistency and repeatability.

2. **Setting Up Ansible**

   o Install Ansible:

   bash

   ```
   sudo apt update
   sudo apt install ansible
   ```

   o Configure the inventory file:

   - Edit /etc/ansible/hosts:

     ini

     ```
     [web]
     server1                 ansible_host=192.168.1.10
     ansible_user=ubuntu
     server2                 ansible_host=192.168.1.11
     ansible_user=ubuntu
     ```

3. **Writing Ansible Playbooks**

   o **Playbook Structure**:

   - YAML format with tasks to execute on target machines.

   o **Example Playbook: Install Apache**:

   yaml

```
---
- hosts: web
  become: yes
  tasks:
    - name: Install Apache
      apt:
        name: apache2
        state: present
    - name: Start Apache service
      service:
        name: apache2
        state: started
```

- o **Run the Playbook**:

bash

```
ansible-playbook apache-install.yml
```

4. **Advanced Ansible Features**
   - o **Roles**:
     - Organize playbooks for complex setups.
   - o **Vault**:
     - Encrypt sensitive data like passwords and keys:

     bash

     ```
     ansible-vault encrypt secrets.yml
     ansible-playbook playbook.yml --ask-vault-pass
     ```

21.4 Practical Examples and Exercises

1. **Examples**

   o Automate a CI/CD pipeline with Jenkins to build and test a Node.js application.

   o Deploy a sample Python web app using GitLab CI/CD and Docker.

   o Use Ansible to configure a load balancer and deploy web servers.

2. **Hands-On Exercises**

   o Write a Jenkinsfile to automate a multi-stage pipeline.

   o Create and test a .gitlab-ci.yml file to deploy an application.

   o Use Ansible to provision a database server and secure it with a firewall.

3. **Common Troubleshooting**

   o Fix Jenkins plugin issues by updating dependencies.

   o Resolve GitLab CI/CD failures by checking .gitlab-ci.yml syntax.

   o Diagnose Ansible errors by running in verbose mode:

   bash

   ansible-playbook playbook.yml -v

21.5

1. **Key Takeaways**
   - o Linux is the backbone of DevOps, enabling seamless integration of tools for automation, CI/CD, and infrastructure management.
   - o Jenkins and GitLab CI/CD pipelines simplify application delivery.
   - o Ansible makes infrastructure provisioning and configuration scalable and repeatable.

2. **Next Steps**
   - o Explore Kubernetes for container orchestration.
   - o Learn advanced Ansible features like dynamic inventories.
   - o Integrate Jenkins and GitLab with monitoring tools for end-to-end DevOps pipelines.

This chapter equips readers with foundational knowledge to use Linux in DevOps workflows, ensuring they can build, deploy, and manage systems efficiently.

Chapter 22: Performance Tuning and Optimization

This chapter focuses on analyzing Linux system performance, optimizing it for specific workloads, and implementing best practices for efficient system administration. Readers will learn to identify bottlenecks and apply techniques to enhance system efficiency.

22.1 Analyzing System Performance with Tools

1. **Key Performance Metrics**
   - **CPU Usage**: Monitors processor workload.
   - **Memory Usage**: Tracks available and used RAM.
   - **Disk I/O**: Monitors read/write operations.
   - **Network Utilization**: Checks data transfer rates.

2. **Using htop for System Monitoring**
   - Install htop:

     bash

     sudo apt install htop

   - Launch htop:

     bash

htop

- o Key Features:
  - ▪ Real-time CPU, memory, and process monitoring.
  - ▪ Navigate processes with arrow keys and filter by name (F4).
  - ▪ Kill a process directly:
    - ▪ Select a process and press F9.

3. **Analyzing Disk I/O with iotop**
   - o Install iotop:

     bash

     sudo apt install iotop

   - o Monitor disk usage:

     bash

     sudo iotop

   - o Key Features:
     - ▪ Identify processes with high disk activity.
     - ▪ Sort processes by disk read/write rates.

4. **Other Performance Monitoring Tools**
   - o **vmstat**: Provides a of CPU, memory, and I/O activity:

bash

vmstat 2 5

- **sar** (System Activity Reporter):
    - Install sysstat:

    bash

    sudo apt install sysstat

    - Collect and display system activity:

    bash

    sar -u 2 5

- **netstat** and **iftop**: Monitor network usage.
    - Example: iftop to display live bandwidth usage:

    bash

    sudo iftop

22.2 Optimizing Linux for Specific Workloads

1. **General Optimization Techniques**
    - **Reduce Background Processes**:

- Disable unnecessary services:

bash

sudo systemctl disable [service_name]

- **Manage Swappiness**:
  - Swappiness determines how often the system uses swap space.
  - Check current swappiness:

bash

cat /proc/sys/vm/swappiness

  - Reduce swappiness for workloads requiring faster memory access:

bash

sudo sysctl vm.swappiness=10

2. **Optimizing for High-Performance Applications**
   - **CPU Optimization**:
     - Use taskset to bind a process to specific CPU cores:

bash

```
taskset -c 0,1 my_program
```

- **Memory Optimization**:
  - Enable hugepages for memory-intensive applications like databases.
  - Configure /etc/sysctl.conf:

    plaintext

    vm.nr_hugepages = 512

  - Apply changes:

    bash

    sudo sysctl -p

3. **Optimizing for Database Workloads**
   - **Tune I/O Scheduler**:
     - Check current scheduler:

       bash

       cat /sys/block/sda/queue/scheduler

     - Set to noop or deadline for better database performance:

       bash

```
echo        deadline      |      sudo      tee
/sys/block/sda/queue/scheduler
```

- o **Use Dedicated Storage**:
  - Assign separate disks for data and logs.
- o **Enable Caching**:
  - Use tools like memcached or Redis for frequently accessed data.

4. **Optimizing for Web Servers**
   - o Enable HTTP/2 for faster response times.
   - o Use a caching proxy like Varnish for static content.
   - o Configure persistent connections in web servers (e.g., Apache, Nginx).

22.3 Best Practices for Efficient System Administration

1. **Regular System Updates**
   - o Keep the system up-to-date to benefit from performance improvements:

   bash

   sudo apt update && sudo apt upgrade

2. **Implement Automated Monitoring**

o   Set up tools like **Prometheus** and **Grafana** for real-time metrics and visualizations.

3. **Scheduled Maintenance Tasks**

o   Automate disk cleanup using cron:

bash

0 2 * * * sudo apt autoclean && sudo apt autoremove

4. **Resource Management**

o   Use cgroups to allocate resources for processes:

▪   Example: Limit CPU usage:

bash

```
cgcreate -g cpu:/mygroup
echo              50000              >
/sys/fs/cgroup/cpu/mygroup/cpu.cfs_quota_us
cgexec -g cpu:/mygroup my_program
```

5. **Logging and Alerts**

o   Centralize logs using tools like ELK Stack (Elasticsearch, Logstash, Kibana).

o   Set up alerts for critical resource thresholds:

▪   Example: Use alertmanager with Prometheus.

6. **Backup and Disaster Recovery**

o   Schedule regular backups with rsync:

bash

rsync -av --progress /data /backup

- o Test recovery procedures periodically.

22.4 Practical Examples and Exercises

1. **Examples**
   - o Monitor and resolve high CPU usage using htop.
   - o Tune the swappiness value to optimize for a memory-intensive workload.
   - o Optimize an Nginx web server for handling concurrent requests.

2. **Hands-On Exercises**
   - o Identify the top I/O-consuming processes with iotop.
   - o Configure sysctl.conf to optimize kernel parameters for a high-performance application.
   - o Create a cron job to clean up old log files automatically.

3. **Common Troubleshooting**
   - o Fix disk bottlenecks by analyzing I/O patterns with iotop.
   - o Resolve system slowdowns by identifying misbehaving processes in htop.

o Address memory leaks by inspecting swap and cache usage.

22.5

1. **Key Takeaways**

   o Tools like htop, iotop, and vmstat provide detailed insights into system performance.

   o Specific workloads, such as databases or web servers, require tailored optimizations.

   o Regular maintenance, monitoring, and resource allocation ensure efficient system administration.

2. **Next Steps**

   o Explore advanced monitoring solutions like Zabbix or Nagios.

   o Learn kernel tuning for specialized environments like real-time applications.

   o Implement containerization (e.g., Docker) to isolate workloads and improve performance.

This chapter equips readers with the knowledge to monitor, analyze, and optimize Linux systems effectively, ensuring maximum performance for any workload.

Chapter 23: Introduction to Cloud Computing with Linux

This chapter introduces cloud computing with Linux, focusing on deploying Linux instances on major cloud platforms like AWS, Azure, and Google Cloud. It also covers managing cloud instances using Linux commands and explores real-world use cases for developers.

23.1 Deploying Linux in the Cloud

1. **Why Use Linux in the Cloud?**
   - Lightweight, secure, and cost-effective.
   - Vast compatibility with cloud services and applications.
   - Dominant OS for servers in cloud environments.

2. **Deploying a Linux Instance on Major Cloud Platforms**
   - **AWS (Amazon Web Services):**
     - Launch an EC2 instance:
       1. Log in to the AWS Management Console.
       2. Navigate to **EC2 → Instances → Launch Instance**.

3. Choose an Amazon Machine Image (AMI), such as Ubuntu or CentOS.

4. Configure instance type, storage, and security groups.

5. Launch the instance and download the private key (.pem file).

- Connect to the instance:

bash

ssh -i "key.pem" ubuntu@ec2-XX-XX-XX-XX.compute-1.amazonaws.com

o **Azure**:

- Deploy a virtual machine:

1. Log in to the Azure Portal.

2. Navigate to **Virtual Machines** → **Create**.

3. Choose an image (e.g., Ubuntu Server) and configure the instance.

4. Generate or use an existing SSH key for access.

- Connect to the instance:

bash

ssh azureuser@XX.XX.XX.XX

- o **Google Cloud Platform (GCP)**:
    - ▪ Launch a Compute Engine instance:
        1. Log in to the GCP Console.
        2. Navigate to **Compute Engine → VM Instances → Create Instance**.
        3. Choose a Linux image, such as Debian or CentOS.
        4. Configure SSH access by adding your public key.
    - ▪ Connect to the instance:

    bash

    ssh username@XX.XX.XX.XX

3. **Choosing the Right Cloud Service**
    - o Factors to consider:
        - ▪ Workload requirements.
        - ▪ Cost and scalability.
        - ▪ Available integrations and services (e.g., databases, AI/ML).

23.2 Managing Cloud Instances with Linux Commands

1. **Basic Instance Management**
    - o **Check Instance Status**:

- **AWS CLI:**

  bash

  ```
  aws ec2 describe-instances --instance-ids instance_id
  ```

- **Azure CLI:**

  bash

  ```
  az vm show --name vm_name --resource-group resource_group
  ```

- **GCP CLI:**

  bash

  ```
  gcloud compute instances describe instance_name
  ```

- **Start and Stop Instances:**
  - **AWS:**

    bash

    ```
    aws ec2 start-instances --instance-ids instance_id
    aws ec2 stop-instances --instance-ids instance_id
    ```

  - **Azure:**

    bash

```
az vm start --name vm_name --resource-group
resource_group
az vm stop --name vm_name --resource-group
resource_group
```

- **GCP:**

```bash
gcloud compute instances start instance_name
gcloud compute instances stop instance_name
```

2. Configuring Instances

o Update and install packages:

```bash
sudo apt update && sudo apt upgrade -y
sudo apt install apache2
```

o Add users and manage SSH keys:

```bash
sudo adduser newuser
sudo usermod -aG sudo newuser
mkdir /home/newuser/.ssh
echo "public_key" >> /home/newuser/.ssh/authorized_keys
chmod 600 /home/newuser/.ssh/authorized_keys
```

3. Monitoring and Troubleshooting

- o **Monitor Resource Usage**:
  - Use top or htop to monitor processes.
  - Install cloud-specific monitoring tools (e.g., AWS CloudWatch Agent):

    bash

    sudo yum install amazon-cloudwatch-agent

- o **Troubleshoot Connection Issues**:
  - Verify security group rules or firewall settings.
  - Use ping to test connectivity to other instances.

4. **Automating Tasks with Cron Jobs**
   - o Schedule regular tasks on cloud instances:

     bash

     crontab -e

     - Example: Automate backups:

       bash

       0 2 * * * tar -czf /backup/$(date +\%Y\%m\%d).tar.gz /data

---

23.3 Real-World Use Cases for Developers

1. **Web Application Hosting**

   o Deploy a LAMP/LEMP stack for hosting applications.

   o Use a reverse proxy like Nginx with SSL termination for security.

   o Example: Deploy a WordPress site on an Ubuntu EC2 instance.

2. **CI/CD Pipelines**

   o Use cloud-hosted instances as runners for CI/CD tools like Jenkins or GitLab.

   o Example: Install Jenkins on an AWS instance:

   bash

   ```
   sudo apt update
   sudo apt install openjdk-11-jdk
   wget -q -O - https://pkg.jenkins.io/debian-stable/jenkins.io.key
   | sudo apt-key add -
   sudo sh -c 'echo deb http://pkg.jenkins.io/debian-stable binary/
   > /etc/apt/sources.list.d/jenkins.list'
   sudo apt update
   sudo apt install jenkins
   ```

3. **Data Processing**

   o Spin up instances to process large datasets.

   o Example: Use a Python script to analyze data in cloud storage:

python

import boto3
s3 = boto3.client('s3')
s3.download_file('mybucket', 'data.csv', 'data.csv')

4. Scaling Applications

- o Use cloud tools for auto-scaling:
  - AWS Auto Scaling Groups.
  - Azure Virtual Machine Scale Sets.
  - GCP Instance Groups.

23.4 Practical Examples and Exercises

1. Examples

- o Deploy a basic web application using an Ubuntu instance on AWS.
- o Automate a daily backup task using a cron job on a cloud instance.
- o Monitor an instance's performance using the AWS CloudWatch Agent.

2. Hands-On Exercises

- o Launch and configure a Linux instance on your preferred cloud platform.
- o Write a script to start and stop instances using the cloud CLI.

o   Set up a simple Nginx reverse proxy on a GCP instance.

3. **Common Troubleshooting**

o   Resolve SSH connection issues by checking key permissions and firewall settings.

o   Fix slow instance performance by resizing the instance type or optimizing workloads.

o   Diagnose startup issues using cloud console logs.

23.5

1. **Key Takeaways**

o   Linux is the preferred OS for cloud computing due to its flexibility and performance.

o   Cloud platforms like AWS, Azure, and GCP provide seamless tools for deploying and managing Linux instances.

o   Real-world use cases, from hosting web applications to scaling services, showcase Linux's utility in the cloud.

2. **Next Steps**

o   Explore container orchestration with Kubernetes on cloud platforms.

- o Learn advanced cloud networking concepts like VPNs and load balancers.
- o Experiment with serverless architectures alongside traditional instances.

This chapter equips readers with the skills to deploy, manage, and utilize Linux in cloud environments effectively, addressing modern developer needs.

Chapter 24: Real-World Project: Building a Development Environment

This chapter guides readers through setting up a complete development environment for web or software development, automating configurations using scripts, and troubleshooting and refining the setup. The goal is to create a reusable and efficient environment tailored to specific development needs.

24.1 Setting Up a Complete Dev Environment for Web or Software Development

1. **Defining the Requirements**

   o Identify the tools and frameworks needed for the project:

      ▪ Programming languages (e.g., Python, JavaScript, Java).

      ▪ Frameworks (e.g., Flask, React, Django).

      ▪ Tools (e.g., Git, Docker, Node.js).

2. **Installing Essential Software**

   o **Package Managers**:

      ▪ Install necessary package managers for software installations:

      bash

```
sudo apt install curl git wget
```

- ○ **Programming Languages**:
  - ▪ Python:

    bash

    ```
    sudo apt install python3 python3-pip
    ```

  - ▪ Node.js:

    bash

    ```
    curl  -fsSL  https://deb.nodesource.com/setup_16.x  |
    sudo -E bash -
    sudo apt install -y nodejs
    ```

  - ▪ Java:

    bash

    ```
    sudo apt install openjdk-11-jdk
    ```

- ○ **Frameworks and Libraries**:
  - ▪ Example: Install Django for Python:

    bash

    ```
    pip install django
    ```

3. **Setting Up a Code Editor or IDE**

   o Install **Visual Studio Code**:

   bash

   sudo apt update
   sudo apt install code

   o Configure IDE extensions:

   - Python, Docker, Prettier, and GitLens extensions for VS Code.

4. **Database Setup**

   o Install and configure a database:

   - MySQL:

   bash

   sudo apt install mysql-server
   sudo mysql_secure_installation

   - PostgreSQL:

   bash

   sudo apt install postgresql postgresql-contrib

5. **Version Control with Git**

   o Configure Git:

bash

git config --global user.name "Your Name"
git config --global user.email "your.email@example.com"

6. **Optional Tools**

   o Docker for containerized development:

   bash

   sudo apt install docker.io
   sudo usermod -aG docker $USER

   o Virtual environments for Python:

   bash

   python3 -m venv env
   source env/bin/activate

24.2 Automating Configurations with Scripts

1. **Why Automate?**

   o Reduces setup time and minimizes human error.

   o Ensures consistency across environments.

2. **Creating a Bash Script for Automation**

   o Example Script: Setting up a Python web development environment.

bash

```
#!/bin/bash

echo "Updating package lists..."
sudo apt update

echo "Installing essential tools..."
sudo apt install -y git curl wget

echo "Installing Python and pip..."
sudo apt install -y python3 python3-pip

echo "Setting up virtual environment..."
python3 -m venv dev_env
source dev_env/bin/activate

echo "Installing Django..."
pip install django

echo "Development environment setup complete!"
```

o   Save the script as setup_dev_env.sh, make it executable, and run it:

bash

```
chmod +x setup_dev_env.sh
./setup_dev_env.sh
```

3. Using Docker Compose for Multi-Service Environments

○ Example docker-compose.yml for a web app:

yaml

```
version: '3.8'
services:
  web:
    image: python:3.9
    volumes:
      - .:/app
    working_dir: /app
    command: python manage.py runserver 0.0.0.0:8000
    ports:
      - "8000:8000"
  db:
    image: postgres
    environment:
      POSTGRES_USER: user
      POSTGRES_PASSWORD: password
      POSTGRES_DB: app_db
```

24.3 Troubleshooting and Refining the Setup

1. Common Issues

○ **Missing Dependencies**:

▪ Check for missing libraries or tools:

bash

sudo apt --fix-broken install

- o **Permission Denied Errors**:
  - Use sudo for administrative tasks or verify user permissions.
- o **Version Conflicts**:
  - Use version managers like pyenv for Python or nvm for Node.js.

2. Testing the Environment

- o Run a sample project:
  - For Python:

bash

```
django-admin startproject testproject
cd testproject
python manage.py runserver
```

  - For Node.js:

bash

```
mkdir testapp
cd testapp
npm init -y
npm install express
```

3. Refining the Setup

- o Optimize for performance:
    - Use tools like Prettier for code formatting and ESLint for linting.
- o Add logging and monitoring tools:
    - Integrate tools like htop for performance monitoring.

4. **Documenting the Setup**

- o Create a README file with setup instructions and scripts:

plaintext

Development Environment Setup
1. Clone the repository.
2. Run `setup_dev_env.sh` to install dependencies.
3. Start the development server with `python manage.py runserver`.

24.4 Practical Examples and Exercises

1. **Examples**
   - o Automate the setup of a Node.js and MongoDB environment using a Bash script.
   - o Create a Docker Compose configuration for a full-stack web application.
   - o Set up a Python virtual environment and install Flask.

2. **Hands-On Exercises**

- o Write a script to configure a development environment for React.js.
- o Build and deploy a simple Dockerized web application.
- o Troubleshoot and fix dependency issues in a provided setup script.

3. Common Troubleshooting

- o Fix environment variable issues by sourcing .bashrc or .zshrc:

bash

```
source ~/.bashrc
```

- o Resolve database connection errors by verifying credentials and ports.
- o Address container startup issues by inspecting logs:

bash

```
docker logs container_id
```

24.5

1. Key Takeaways

- o Setting up a development environment involves installing necessary tools, configuring the system, and automating repetitive tasks.
- o Scripts and tools like Docker Compose simplify and standardize environment setups.
- o Troubleshooting skills ensure a seamless and efficient development experience.

2. **Next Steps**

- o Explore advanced container orchestration with Kubernetes.
- o Learn to use cloud-based development environments like GitHub Codespaces.
- o Experiment with hybrid setups combining local and cloud development environments.

This chapter provides a hands-on approach to building and managing development environments, ensuring readers can streamline their workflows and focus on coding.

Chapter 25: The Future of Linux in Programming

This chapter explores the future of Linux in programming, highlighting emerging trends, the growth of open-source contributions, and actionable next steps for readers to continue their Linux and programming journey.

25.1 Emerging Trends in Linux for Developers

1. **Containerization and Cloud-Native Development**
   - The dominance of Linux in powering containerization platforms like **Docker** and orchestration tools like **Kubernetes**.
   - The rise of **serverless computing** and how Linux supports serverless platforms (e.g., AWS Lambda, Azure Functions).
   - Integration of Linux with edge computing for IoT and low-latency applications.

2. **Linux and AI/ML Development**
   - **TensorFlow, PyTorch**, and other popular AI/ML frameworks are optimized for Linux.
   - Support for GPU acceleration on Linux through tools like **CUDA** and **Rocm**.

o Linux as the default OS for AI researchers and data scientists using cloud-based Jupyter notebooks and distributed training.

3. **Linux for Cross-Platform Development**

o Growth of tools like **WSL (Windows Subsystem for Linux)** enabling Linux environments on Windows for seamless cross-platform development.

o **Flatpak** and **Snap** packages simplify distributing Linux-based desktop applications across multiple distributions.

4. **Linux in DevOps and Automation**

o Increasing adoption of **Infrastructure as Code (IaC)** with tools like Ansible, Terraform, and Chef, which are primarily Linux-based.

o Linux's critical role in CI/CD pipelines for deploying modern applications.

5. **Linux in Security-Centric Development**

o Growth of **Cybersecurity tools** on Linux, including Kali Linux for penetration testing and Linux-based firewalls.

o Linux as a primary platform for blockchain development and decentralized apps (dApps).

25.2 Growth of Open-Source Contributions

1. **The Open-Source Movement**
   - o Linux is the foundation of the open-source software ecosystem.
   - o Developers contributing to Linux kernel projects, distributions (e.g., Ubuntu, Fedora), and applications.

2. **Community-Driven Development**
   - o Platforms like **GitHub, GitLab**, and **SourceForge** have accelerated open-source collaboration.
   - o Initiatives like the **Linux Foundation** and **Open Source Summit** continue to foster innovation and inclusivity.

3. **Opportunities for Developers**
   - o Contribute to Linux-based projects in languages like C, Python, and Rust.
   - o Develop tools or frameworks that improve Linux usability or performance.
   - o Participate in open-source mentoring programs like **Google Summer of Code**.

4. **Sustainability in Open Source**
   - o Efforts to fund open-source projects through sponsorships, crowd-funding, or corporate partnerships (e.g., GitHub Sponsors).
   - o Growing recognition of open-source maintainers' efforts in the developer community.

25.3 Final Thoughts and Next Steps for Readers

1. **The Enduring Relevance of Linux**

   o   Linux remains the foundation for innovation in software development.

   o   Its adaptability ensures it will continue thriving in emerging fields like cloud computing, AI, and IoT.

2. **Embrace Continuous Learning**

   o   Stay updated with Linux-related technologies by following blogs, forums, and Linux communities.

   o   Experiment with advanced Linux topics like kernel development or real-time operating systems.

3. **Get Hands-On Experience**

   o   Build real-world projects, such as containerized applications or automated deployment pipelines.

   o   Contribute to open-source projects to improve skills and network with like-minded developers.

4. **Expand Horizons**

   o   Explore advanced tools like Kubernetes for orchestration and SELinux for security.

   o   Dive into Linux-based development for blockchain, AI, or IoT.

Practical Exercises and Next Steps

1. **Exercises**

   o Research and contribute to an open-source Linux project of your choice.

   o Create a simple automation script or CI/CD pipeline for a personal project.

   o Set up a Linux-based cloud environment using Docker or Kubernetes.

2. **Suggested Learning Resources**

   o **Books**: *The Linux Programming Interface* by Michael Kerrisk.

   o **Courses**: FreeCodeCamp's Linux tutorials or Linux Foundation training courses.

   o **Communities**: Join Linux-related subreddits, forums, or local user groups.

25.4

1. **Key Takeaways**

   o Linux is integral to the future of programming, from DevOps to AI to security.

   o Open-source contributions drive innovation and are an excellent way for developers to grow their skills and impact.

o   Mastering Linux tools and technologies opens doors to advanced career opportunities.

2. **Next Steps**

o   Keep experimenting with Linux tools and projects.

o   Contribute to the vibrant open-source community.

o   Stay informed about emerging trends and technologies that build on Linux.

www.ingramcontent.com/pod-product-compliance
Lightning Source LLC
La Vergne TN
LVHW022341060326
832902LV00022B/4171